THE SCHOOL MATHEMATICS PROJECT

When the S.M.P. was founded in 1961, its objective was to devise radically new mathematics courses, with accompanying G.C.E. syllabuses and examinations, which would reflect, more adequately than did the traditional syllabuses, the up-to-date nature and usages of mathematics.

The first stage of this objective is now more or less complete. *Books 1–5* form the main series of pupils' texts, starting at the age of 11+ and leading to the O-level examination in 'S.M.P. Mathematics', while *Books 3T*, 4* and *5* give a three-year course to the same O-level examination. (*Books T* and *T4*, together with their Supplement, represent the first attempt at this three-year course, but they may be regarded as obsolete.) *Advanced Mathematics Books 1–4* cover the syllabus for the A-level examination in 'S.M.P. Mathematics' and in preparation are five (or more) shorter texts covering the material of various sections of the A-level examination in 'S.M.P. Further Mathematics'. There are two books for 'S.M.P. Additional Mathematics' at O-level. Every book is accompanied by a Teacher's Guide.

For the convenience of schools, the S.M.P. has an arrangement whereby its examinations are made available by every G.C.E. Examining Board, and it is most grateful to the Secretaries of the eight Boards for their cooperation in this. At the same time, most Boards now offer their own syllabuses in 'modern mathematics' for which the S.M.P. texts are suitable.

By 1967, it had become clear from experience in comprehensive schools that the mathematical content of the S.M.P. texts was suitable for a much wider range of pupil than had been originally anticipated, but that the presentation needed adaptation. Thus it was decided to produce a new series, *Books A–H*, which could serve as a secondary-school course starting at the age of 11+. These books are specially suitable for pupils aiming at a C.S.E. examination; however, the framework of the C.S.E. examinations is such that it is inappropriate for the S.M.P. to offer its own examination as it does for the G.C.E.

The completion of all these books does not mean that the S.M.P. has no more to offer to the cause of curriculum research. The team of S.M.P. writers, now numbering some thirty school and university mathematicians, is continually testing and revising old work and preparing for new. At the same time, the effectiveness of the S.M.P.'s work depends, as it always has done, on obtaining reactions from active teachers—and also from pupils—in the classroom. Readers of the texts can therefore send their comments to the S.M.P. in the knowledge that they will be warmly welcomed.

Finally, the year-by-year activity of the S.M.P. is recorded in the annual Director's Reports which readers are encouraged to obtain on request to the S.M.P. Office at Westfield College, University of London, Kidderpore Avenue, London N.W.3.

* *Book 3T* to be published in 1970 by Cambridge University Press.

ACKNOWLEDGEMENTS

The principal authors, on whose contributions the S.M.P. texts are largely based, are named in the annual Reports. Many other authors have also provided original material, and still more have been directly involved in the revision of draft versions of chapters and books. The Project gratefully acknowledges the contributions which they and their schools have made.

This book—*Book D*—has been written by

Joyce Harris	R. A. Parsons
Christine Hopkins	C. Richards
D. A. Hobbs	R. W. Strong
K. Lewis	Thelma Wilson

and edited by Elizabeth Evans.

The Project owes much to its Secretaries, Miss Jacqueline Sinfield and Mrs Jennifer Whittaker for their willing assistance and careful typing in connection with this book.

We would especially thank Dr J. V. Armitage for the advice he has given on the fundamental mathematics of the course.

The drawings at the chapter openings in this book are by Penny Wager.

The Project is grateful to the Royal Mint for supplying the photograph of the 50p coin.

We are much indebted to the Cambridge University Press for their cooperation and help at all times in the preparation of this book.

THE SCHOOL MATHEMATICS PROJECT

BOOK D

CAMBRIDGE
AT THE UNIVERSITY PRESS

1969

10/‒
HN

Published by the Syndics of the Cambridge University Press
Bentley House, 200 Euston Road, London N.W. 1
American Branch: 32 East 57th Street, New York, N.Y. 10022

© Cambridge University Press 1969

Library of Congress Catalogue Card Number: 68–21399
Standard Book Number: 521 07589 0

Printed in Great Britain
at the University Printing House, Cambridge
(Brooke Crutchley, University Printer)

Preface

This is the fourth of eight books designed to cover a course suitable for those who wish to take a C.S.E. examination on one of the reformed mathematics syllabuses.

The material is based upon the first four books of the O-level series, S.M.P. *Books 1–4*. The connection is maintained to the extent that it will be possible to change from one series to the other at the end of the first year or even at a later stage. For example, having started with *Books A* and *B*, a pupil will be able to move to *Book 2*. Within each year's work, the material has been entirely broken down and rewritten.

The differences between this Main School series and the O-level series have been explained at length in the Preface to *Book A* as have the differences between the content of these two S.M.P. courses and that of the more traditional text.

In this book, *Book D*, the Prelude provides informal work on the properties of group tables by means of carefully graded experiments. The ideas of identity and inverse were briefly introduced in *Book C* in connection with 'shifts', but the Prelude shows them in a wider setting and introduces, for the first time, the idea of closure. Associativity will be discussed in Chapter 5, and this chapter also introduces some algebraic conventions and provides practice in simple algebraic manipulation.

Book D contains four chapters on arithmetic. The first two deal with multiplication and division of fractions and directed numbers respectively, and complete the basic work to be done in this course on fractions and directed numbers. The last two chapters are concerned with ratios and percentages. (There will be more work on these two topics later in the course.)

Enlargement is a transformation that preserves shape but not size. The chapter which deals with this contains mainly practical work, but the ideas of the chapter will be drawn on in *Book E* to serve as an introduction to trigonometry and again in later work on similarity. In this book also, the powerful concept of a vector is introduced together with further work on translations and their combination.

The work on symmetry done in *Books A* and *C* is completed in *Book D* with a chapter on three-dimensional rotational symmetry. In addition, there is a considerable amount of graphical work in *Book D*, and the number patterns to be found in Pascal's Triangle and the Fibonacci Sequence are investigated.

Answers to exercises are not printed at the end of this book but are contained in the companion Teacher's Guide which gives a detailed commentary on the pupil's text. In this series, the answers and commentary are inter-leaved with the text.

Contents

Contents

Prelude

LOOKING AT TABLES
Experiment 1

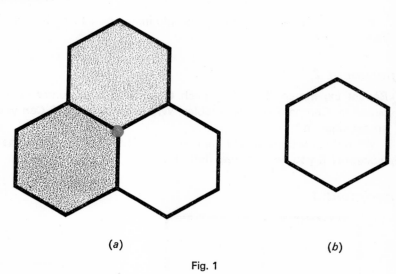

(a)   (b)

Fig. 1

Instruction *A* means   leave your counter where it is.

Instruction *B* means   rotate your counter about the red dot through $\frac{1}{3}$ turn anticlockwise.

Instruction *C* means   rotate your counter about the red dot through $\frac{1}{3}$ turn clockwise.

Trace Figure 1 (*b*) and cut out a hexagonal counter. Starting each time with your counter on the white hexagon in Figure 1 (*a*), find out where your counter would land after each of the following pairs of instructions:

(i) *B* followed by *C*; (ii) *C* followed by *A*; (iii) *B* followed by *B*.

After *B* followed by *C* your counter lands on the white hexagon. This result could be obtained more simply by using instruction *A*, so we could say that

B followed by *C* gives *A*.

Is it possible to replace the other two pairs of instructions by a single instruction? (Remember to start from the white hexagon each time.)

1

Copy and complete this table:

First instruction	Followed by	Second instruction A	B	C
	A			
	B		C	A
	C	C		

Were you always able to find a single instruction to replace a pair of instructions?

Experiment 2

Repeat Experiment 1 starting each time with your counter on the red hexagon. Compare your two tables. What do you notice? Can you give an explanation?

What do you think would happen if you always started from the black hexagon? If you are not sure, find out.

Experiment 3

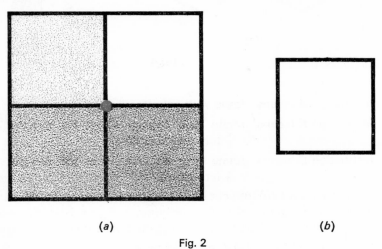

(a)   (b)

Fig. 2

Instruction *P* means   leave your counter where it is.

Instruction *Q* means   rotate your counter about the red dot through $\frac{1}{4}$ turn anticlockwise.

Instruction *R* means   rotate your counter about the red dot through $\frac{1}{4}$ turn clockwise.

Trace Figure 2 (*b*) and cut out a square counter. Copy the following table and see whether you can complete it:

	Followed by	Second instruction P	Q	R
	P		Q	
First instruction	Q			P
	R			

Were you always able to find a single instruction to replace a pair of instructions?

1. CLOSURE

In Experiments 1 and 2, the members of the set {*A, B, C*} can always be combined by the operation 'followed by' to give a result which belongs to this set. Since it is possible to complete the combination table using only the members of the given set, we say that the set {*A, B, C*} is *closed* under the operation 'followed by'.

In Experiment 3, we cannot complete the combination table using only members of the set {*P, Q, R*}. We say that the set {*P, Q, R*} is not closed under 'followed by'.

Experiment 4

P, Q, R have the meanings which they had in Experiment 3. Describe instruction *S* so that the set {*P, Q, R, S*} is closed under the operation 'followed by' and complete a copy of this table:

	Followed by	Second instruction P	Q	R	S
	P	P	Q	R	
First instruction	Q	Q		P	
	R	R	P		
	S				

Experiment 5

For this experiment you will need four cards *A*, *B*, *C*, *D* with rectangular holes like those in Figure 3.

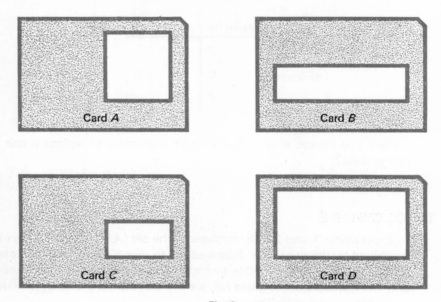

Fig. 3

Place card *A* on top of card *B*. (Make sure that you have not turned the cards round or turned them over.) You now have a hole which matches the hole in card *C*. We can say that

card *A* placed on top of card *B* gives the same result as card *C*.

Copy and complete this table:

		Placed on top of	Second card			
			A	*B*	*C*	*D*
		A		*C*		
First		*B*				
card		*C*				
		D				

Is the set {*A*, *B*, *C*, *D*} closed under 'placed on top of'?

Suppose that you are now given another card *E*, shown in Figure 4. Is the set {*A, B, C, D, E*} closed under 'placed on top of'?

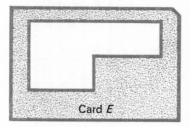

Fig. 4

Try to find a new set such that *A, B, C, D* and *E* are members of this set and such that the new set is closed under 'placed on top of'.

Make the new cards which you require and a combination table for the new set.

2. IDENTITY

Look again at the combination table which you obtained from Experiment 1 :

		Second instruction		
Followed by		*A*	*B*	*C*
	A	*A*	*B*	*C*
First instruction	*B*	*B*	*C*	*A*
	C	*C*	*A*	*B*

We see that :

A followed by *A* gives *A*,

A followed by *B* gives *B*,

A followed by *C* gives *C*,

B followed by *A* gives *B*,

C followed by *A* gives *C*.

Combination with *A*, whether *A* is the first or the second instruction, has no effect. Since any member of the set remains unchanged when combined with *A*, we say that *A* is the *identity* for this set.

Look at the tables you obtained from Experiments 3, 4, 5 and decide what is the identity in each case.

What is the identity when ordinary numbers are (i) added, (ii) multiplied ?

5

Find the identity in the following table for the operation ∗ on the set {K, L, M, N}:

	Second member			
∗	K	L	M	N
K	M	N	K	L
L	N	K	L	M
M	K	L	M	N
N	L	M	N	K

First member (rows labelled K, L, M, N)

Experiment 6

Cottage, palace, mansion, pigsty, cottage, palace, ... is a rhyme which is sometimes used for counting plumstones.

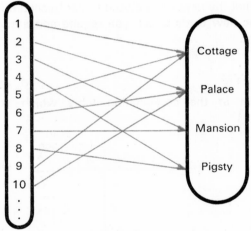

Fig. 5

The arrow diagram in Figure 5 shows the mapping from the set {1, 2, 3, 4, ...} onto the set {cottage, palace, mansion, pigsty}.

The table in Figure 6 gives the same information:

Cottage	Palace	Mansion	Pigsty
1	2	3	4
5	6	7	8
9	10	·	·
·	·	·	·
·	·	·	·
·	·		·

Fig. 6

Copy this table and add several more numbers to each column. You may assume that you have a large supply of stones.

Suppose you have two helpings of plums: one with 5 stones and one with 3. How many stones do you have altogether?

$$
\begin{array}{lcl}
5 & \longrightarrow & \text{Cottage} \\
3 & \longrightarrow & \text{Mansion} \\
8 & \longrightarrow & \text{Pigsty}
\end{array}
$$

We could say that cottage followed by mansion gives pigsty.

Choose two other numbers, one from the column headed cottage and one from the column headed mansion and add them together. In which column is your answer? Try other pairs of numbers. Can we always say that cottage followed by mansion gives pigsty?

Suppose you now choose two numbers, one from the column headed mansion and one from the column headed palace and add them together. Where is your answer? Is it always in the same column no matter which numbers you choose?

Copy the following table and find out if it is possible to complete it:

		Second member			
	Followed by	Cottage	Palace	Mansion	Pigsty
First member	Cottage			Pigsty	
	Palace				
	Mansion		Cottage		
	Pigsty				

Is the set {cottage, palace, mansion, pigsty} closed under 'followed by'? Is there an identity? If so, say which member it is. If not, give a reason.

Use your table to find which member of the set ? must be if:

(i) cottage followed by ? gives pigsty;

(ii) ? followed by palace gives pigsty.

7

3. INVERSES

(*a*) Look again at the combination table which you obtained from Experiment 4:

	Followed by	P	Q	R	S
		Second instruction			
First instruction	P	ⓟ	Q	R	S
	Q	Q	S	ⓟ	R
	R	R	ⓟ	S	Q
	S	S	R	Q	ⓟ

The identity is *P* and four pairs of instructions combine to give the identity:

$$P \text{ followed by } P \text{ gives } P,$$
$$Q \text{ followed by } R \text{ gives } P,$$
$$R \text{ followed by } Q \text{ gives } P,$$
$$S \text{ followed by } S \text{ gives } P.$$

When two members of a set can be combined in either order to give the identity, they are called *inverses* of each other.

In Experiment 4, *Q* is the inverse of *R* and *R* is the inverse of *Q*; we say that *Q* and *R* are an *inverse pair*.

S is the inverse of itself and we say that *S* is *self-inverse*. What can you say about *P*? Is it self-inverse?

(*b*) Now look again at the combination table which you obtained from Experiment 1:

	Followed by	A	B	C
		Second instruction		
First instruction	A	A	B	C
	B	B	C	A
	C	C	A	B

We have already seen that A is the identity.

Which instruction is self-inverse?

The other two instructions form an inverse pair. Can you see why this is so?

(c) Find your table for Experiment 6.

   (i) Which member of the set {cottage, palace, mansion, pigsty} is the identity?

   (ii) Which members are self-inverse?

   (iii) Which members form an inverse pair?

(d) For each of your tables in Experiment 5, say

   (i) whether there is an identity;

   (ii) which cards, if any, are self-inverse;

   (iii) which cards, if any, are inverse pairs;

   (iv) which cards, if any, have no inverse.

(e) Look at the following table for the operation $*$ on the set $\{a, b, c\}$:

	*	a	b	c
		Second member		
First member	a	a	c	b
	b	c	b	a
	c	b	a	c

Is the set $\{a, b, c\}$ closed under $*$?

Does the set contain an identity?

Does each member of the set have an inverse? Give a reason for your answer.

Experiment 7

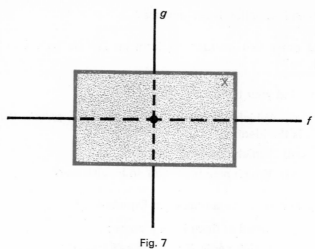

Fig. 7

There are four transformations (changes of position) which map the rectangle onto itself.

Transformation *F* means reflect the rectangle in the line of symmetry, *f*:

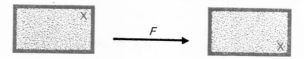

Transformation *G* means reflect the rectangle in the line of symmetry, *g*:

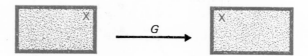

Transformation *H* means rotate through a half-turn about the black dot:

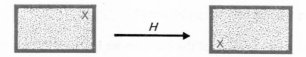

Transformation *I* means leave the rectangle where it is:

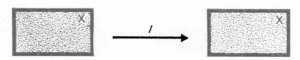

Figure 8 shows that transformation *F* followed by transformation *G* is equivalent to the single transformation *H*.

Fig. 8

Cut a rectangle from card or paper and mark one corner of the rectangle on both sides with a cross. Start always from the position shown in Figure 7 and use your rectangle to help you to complete a copy of this table:

		Second transformation			
	Followed by	*F*	*G*	*H*	*I*
	F		*H*		
First	*G*				
transformation	*H*				
	I				

Is the set {*F, G, H, I*} closed under the operation 'followed by'?
Is there an identity? If so, what is it?
What are the inverses, if any, of *F, G, H, I*?

Experiment 8

Fig. 9

Describe two transformations which map the triangle in Figure 9 onto itself.

Using letters to stand for these transformations, construct a table for the operation 'followed by'. Is the set closed under this operation? Is there an identity? What are the inverses (if any)?

Experiment 9

Make two cards X and Y with numbers front and back as shown in Figure 10.

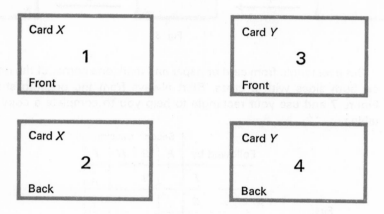

Fig. 10

Place them on your desk like this:

Fig. 11

Instruction A means leave the cards as they are.
Instruction B means reverse both cards (that is turn them over).
Instruction C means reverse card X.
Instruction D means reverse card Y.

Instruction A gives the code number 13 and instruction B gives the code number 24. What code numbers are given by instructions C and D?

If * means 'followed by', C * D gives the number 24, and therefore we can write C * D = B.
What number is given by B * D?
What number is given by C * B?

Copy and complete this table:

	Second instruction			
*	A	B	C	D
A			C	
B		A		
C				B
D				

First instruction

Can you complete the table using only members of $\{A, B, C, D\}$?
Is the set closed under $*$?
What is special about the member A?
Which members are self-inverse?
Find which instruction $?$ must be if:

(i) $? * B = A$;

(ii) $? * C = B$;

(iii) $D * ? = C$;

(iv) $B * ? = D$.

Make up some more equations like these. Can you always find answers?

Experiment 10

Arthur, Brian and Charles are triplets. They should sit in their class in this order: Arthur, Brian, Charles,

but sometimes they change places in order to confuse their teachers. The six cards in Figure 12 show how they do this.

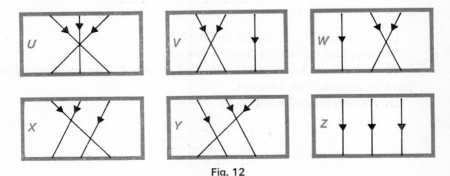

Fig. 12

Make some cards like this and label them U, V, W, X, Y, Z. In how many different orders can the triplets sit?

13

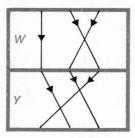 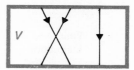

Fig. 13

After move W followed by move Y, they are in the same order as if they had just made move V. Do you agree? (Look at Figure 13.) We shall write this for short as $W \circ Y = V$.

Use your cards to find out whether other pairs of moves can be combined to give a single move. Enter your results in a copy of this table:

		Second move					
$\circ$		U	V	W	X	Y	Z
	U						U
	V						
First move	W			Z		V	
	X						
	Y						
	Z			X			

Is $\{U, V, W, X, Y, Z\}$ closed under $\circ$?

Can you find an identity for $\circ$ in this set?

Write down the inverses of U, V, W, X, Y and Z. If any of them do not have an inverse, give a reason.

Find which move $?$ must be if:

(a) $X \circ ? = Z$;
(b) $? \circ Y = V$;
(c) $? \circ U = X$;
(d) $Y \circ ? = W$.

Make up some more equations like these. Can you always find an answer?

Experiment 11

Fig. 14

Place three pennies on a table, with the centre one showing a tail, and the others showing a head.

You are allowed to turn over any two of the pennies, but always turn just two at a time. Experiment to see if you can do this so that all three finish showing heads.

Make a drawing of each of the possible situations at which you can arrive, remembering to turn over only two pennies at a time. Make your drawings like this:

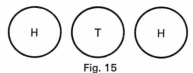

Fig. 15

Give a name to each possible move, starting each time from the position shown in Figure 15. For example, you could leave the pennies as they are to give the identity move:

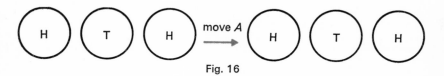

Fig. 16

or you could turn over the first two pennies to give:

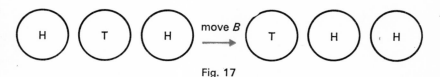

Fig. 17

You should be able to find four different moves. Call then *A*, *B*, *C* and *D*. Moves *A* and *B* are shown in Figures 16 and 17. Draw diagrams of your own to show moves *C* and *D*.

15

Combine these moves under the operation 'followed by' and show your results in a table.

Discuss whether:

(*a*) your table shows closure;

(*b*) your set of moves contains an identity;

(*c*) each member of {*A, B, C, D*} has an inverse;

(*d*) equations like '*A* followed by ? = *B*' always have a solution.

Are you now sure that it is impossible to obtain three heads? Why?

1. Multiplication and division of fractions

1. MULTIPLICATION OF FRACTIONS

1.1 Multiplication of a fraction by a whole number

Multiplication is repeated addition. So, for example,

$$4 \times 5 \text{ is the same as } 4 + 4 + 4 + 4 + 4.$$

Explain why each of the following statements is true:

(a) $\frac{1}{10} \times 3 = \frac{1}{10} + \frac{1}{10} + \frac{1}{10} = \frac{3}{10}$;

(b) $\frac{1}{10} \times 3 = 3 \times \frac{1}{10}$;

(c) $\frac{3}{10} \times 5 = \frac{3}{10} + \frac{3}{10} + \frac{3}{10} + \frac{3}{10} + \frac{3}{10} = \frac{15}{10} (= \frac{3}{2} = 1\frac{1}{2})$;

(d) $\frac{3}{10} \times 5 = 5 \times \frac{3}{10}$.

Is it true that:

(e) $\frac{3}{4} \times 5 = \frac{3}{4} + \frac{3}{4} + \frac{3}{4} + \frac{3}{4} + \frac{3}{4} = \frac{15}{4}$;

(f) $\frac{3}{4} \times 5 = 5 \times \frac{3}{4}$?

17

Multiplication and division of fractions

Exercise A

1 Copy and complete the following. (The first one has been done for you.)

(a)

$\frac{1}{2} \times 6$

$= $

$= 3$

(b)

$\frac{3}{4} \times 4$

$=$

$=$

(c)

$=$

$=$

(d)

$=$

$=$

(e)

$=$

$=$

Work out the following:

2   (a) $\frac{1}{2} \times 8$;   (b) $8 \times \frac{1}{2}$;   (c) $\frac{1}{2}$ of 8;   (d) $8 \div 2$.

3   (a) $\frac{1}{3} \times 9$;   (b) $9 \times \frac{1}{3}$;   (c) $\frac{1}{3}$ of 9;   (d) $9 \div 3$.

4   (a) $\frac{1}{5} \times 15$;   (b) $15 \times \frac{1}{5}$;   (c) $\frac{1}{5}$ of 15;   (d) $15 \div 5$.

5   (a) $\frac{1}{4} \times 5$;   (b) $5 \times \frac{1}{4}$;   (c) $\frac{1}{4}$ of 5;   (d) $5 \div 4$.

6   (a) $\frac{1}{5} \times 4$;   (b) $4 \times \frac{1}{5}$;   (c) $\frac{1}{5}$ of 4;   (d) $4 \div 5$.

7   (a) $\frac{1}{6} \times 9$;   (b) $9 \times \frac{1}{6}$;   (c) $\frac{1}{6}$ of 9;   (d) $9 \div 6$.

8   (a) $\frac{2}{3} \times 6$;   (b) $6 \times \frac{2}{3}$;   (c) $\frac{2}{3}$ of 6.

9   (a) $\frac{3}{4} \times 8$;   (b) $8 \times \frac{3}{4}$;   (c) $\frac{3}{4}$ of 8.

10 (a) $\frac{3}{2} \times 10$;   (b) $10 \times \frac{3}{2}$;   (c) $\frac{3}{2}$ of 10.

11 (a) $\frac{3}{5} \times 7$;   (b) $7 \times \frac{3}{5}$;   (c) $\frac{3}{5}$ of 7.

1.2 Multiplication of a fraction by a fraction

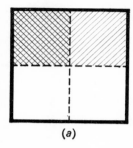 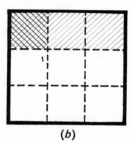

(a)   (b)

Fig. 1

Figure 1 (a) shows $\frac{1}{2}$ of $\frac{1}{2}$ of a square or $\frac{1}{4}$ of a square and

Figure 1 (b) shows $\frac{1}{3}$ of $\frac{1}{3}$ of a square or $\frac{1}{9}$ of a square.

Draw a similar diagram to show $\frac{1}{4}$ of $\frac{1}{4}$ of a square. What fraction is this of the whole square?

What are: (a) $\frac{1}{2} \times \frac{1}{2}$; (b) $\frac{1}{3} \times \frac{1}{3}$; (c) $\frac{1}{4} \times \frac{1}{4}$?

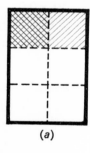 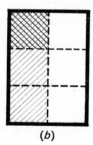

(a)   (b)

Fig. 2

Figure 2 (a) shows that $\frac{1}{2}$ of $\frac{1}{3}$ of a rectangle $= \frac{1}{6}$ of a rectangle, or more simply,

$$\frac{1}{3} \times \frac{1}{2} = \frac{1}{6}.$$

Figure 2 (b) shows that $\frac{1}{3}$ of $\frac{1}{2}$ of a rectangle $= \frac{1}{6}$ of a rectangle, or more simply,

$$\frac{1}{2} \times \frac{1}{3} = \frac{1}{6}.$$

19

Exercise B

1 Draw diagrams to show that:

$$(a) \; \tfrac{1}{2} \text{ of } \tfrac{2}{3} = \tfrac{2}{6} = \tfrac{1}{3};$$

$$(b) \; \tfrac{2}{3} \text{ of } \tfrac{1}{2} = \tfrac{2}{6} = \tfrac{1}{3}.$$

What multiplications have you just illustrated?

2 Draw diagrams to show that:

$(a) \; \tfrac{3}{4} \times \tfrac{1}{3} = \tfrac{3}{12} = \tfrac{1}{4};$ $(c) \; \tfrac{1}{3} \times \tfrac{2}{5} = \tfrac{2}{15};$

$(b) \; \tfrac{1}{3} \times \tfrac{3}{4} = \tfrac{3}{12} = \tfrac{1}{4};$ $(d) \; \tfrac{2}{5} \times \tfrac{1}{3} = \tfrac{2}{15}.$

3 (a) Work out the following, drawing diagrams to help you if necessary.

     (i) $\tfrac{1}{5} \times \tfrac{1}{2}$;   (ii) $\tfrac{1}{5} \times \tfrac{2}{3}$;   (iii) $\tfrac{3}{4} \times \tfrac{1}{5}$;

     (iv) $\tfrac{2}{3} \times \tfrac{3}{5}$;   (v) $\tfrac{1}{8} \times \tfrac{2}{3}$;   (vi) $\tfrac{1}{10} \times \tfrac{3}{4}$.

(b) Explain, in your own words, how to multiply two fractions together.

4 Work out the following:

$(a) \; \tfrac{3}{2} \times \tfrac{2}{3}$; $(b) \; \tfrac{2}{5} \times \tfrac{5}{2}$; $(c) \; \tfrac{3}{11} \times \tfrac{11}{3}$.

You should get the answer 1 each time. Why is this so?

5 You know that:

$(a) \; 0{\cdot}1 \times 0{\cdot}1 = 0{\cdot}01;$ $(b) \; 0{\cdot}1 \times 0{\cdot}01 = 0{\cdot}001;$
$(c) \; 0{\cdot}6 \times 0{\cdot}4 = 0{\cdot}24;$ $(d) \; 0{\cdot}07 \times 0{\cdot}2 = 0{\cdot}014.$

Convert each of these multiplications to fraction form and check that your rule from Question 3 works.

6 Work out the following, giving your answers in their simplest form.

$(a) \; \tfrac{1}{2} \times \tfrac{1}{8}$; $(b) \; \tfrac{1}{4} \times \tfrac{3}{2}$; $(c) \; \tfrac{7}{8} \times \tfrac{1}{3}$; $(d) \; \tfrac{1}{2} \times \tfrac{1}{3} \times \tfrac{1}{4}$;

$(e) \; \tfrac{3}{2} \times \tfrac{3}{4}$; $(f) \; \tfrac{2}{5} \text{ of } \tfrac{3}{10}$; $(g) \; \tfrac{5}{6} \text{ of } \tfrac{2}{3}$; $(h) \; \tfrac{3}{4} \text{ of } \tfrac{7}{10}$;

$(i) \; \tfrac{7}{8} \times 2\tfrac{2}{3}$; $(j) \; \tfrac{3}{10} \times 1\tfrac{1}{6}$; $(k) \; \tfrac{3}{20} \times \tfrac{10}{11} \times 2$; $(l) \; \tfrac{8}{15} \times \tfrac{5}{4} \times \tfrac{3}{2}$.

7 If a and b are positive whole numbers and $b > a$, state whether the following are true or false.

$(a) \; a \times \tfrac{1}{2} < a$; $(b) \; b \times \tfrac{3}{2} < b$; $(c) \; a \times \tfrac{5}{4} > a$;

$(d) \; \dfrac{a}{b} > 1$; $(e) \; \dfrac{a}{b} \times \dfrac{1}{2} > \dfrac{a}{b}$; $(f) \; \dfrac{b}{a} > \dfrac{a}{b}$;

$(g) \; \dfrac{b}{a} \times 1 > \dfrac{b}{a}$; $(h) \; \dfrac{b}{a} \times \dfrac{2}{3} < \dfrac{b}{a}$.

2. DIVISION OF FRACTIONS

2.1 Division of a whole number by a fraction

Copy and complete the following:

(a) $8 \div 2 = \dfrac{8}{?} = 4$;

(b) $8 \div ? = \frac{8}{3} = 2\frac{2}{3}$;

(c) $8 \div \dfrac{1}{2} = \dfrac{8}{\frac{1}{2}} = \dfrac{8 \times ?}{\frac{1}{2} \times 2} = \dfrac{16}{1} = 16$;

(d) $6 \div \dfrac{2}{3} = \dfrac{6}{\frac{2}{3}} = \dfrac{6 \times 3}{\frac{2}{3} \times ?} = \dfrac{18}{?} = ?$;

(e) $12 \div \dfrac{3}{4} = \dfrac{12}{\frac{3}{4}} = \dfrac{12 \times ?}{\frac{3}{4} \times ?} = \dfrac{48}{3} = ?$;

(f) $9 \div \dfrac{4}{5} = \dfrac{9}{\frac{4}{5}} = \dfrac{9 \times ?}{\frac{4}{5} \times ?} = \dfrac{45}{?} = ?$.

Exercise C

1 (a) $5 \div 3$;   (b) $5 \div \frac{1}{3}$;   (c) $4 \div \frac{2}{3}$;   (d) $1 \div \frac{1}{2}$;

(e) $1 \div \frac{3}{5}$;   (f) $6 \div \frac{3}{4}$;   (g) $8 \div \frac{2}{3}$;   (h) $4 \div \frac{2}{5}$;

(i) $6 \div \frac{3}{10}$;   (j) $10 \div \frac{3}{4}$;   (k) $8 \div \frac{3}{2}$;   (l) $5 \div \frac{2}{3}$.

2.2 Division of one fraction by another fraction

Copy and complete the following:

(a) $\dfrac{5}{7} \div \dfrac{2}{7} = \dfrac{\frac{5}{7}}{\frac{2}{7}} = \dfrac{\frac{5}{7} \times 7}{\frac{2}{7} \times 7} = ?$;

(b) $\dfrac{1}{3} \div \dfrac{2}{3} = \dfrac{\frac{1}{3}}{?} = \dfrac{\frac{1}{3} \times 3}{?} = ?$;

(c) $\dfrac{5}{6} \div \dfrac{1}{3} = \dfrac{\frac{5}{6}}{\frac{1}{3}} = \dfrac{\frac{5}{6} \times 6}{\frac{1}{3} \times ?} = \dfrac{5}{2} = 2\frac{1}{2}$;

(d) $\dfrac{3}{2} \div \dfrac{1}{10} = \dfrac{\frac{3}{2}}{\frac{1}{10}} = \dfrac{\frac{3}{2} \times ?}{\frac{1}{10} \times ?} = \dfrac{\frac{30}{2}}{1} = 15$;

(e) $\dfrac{2}{3} \div \dfrac{3}{4} = \dfrac{\frac{2}{3}}{\frac{3}{4}} = \dfrac{\frac{2}{3} \times 12}{\frac{3}{4} \times ?} = \dfrac{\frac{24}{3}}{\frac{36}{4}} = \dfrac{8}{9}$;

(f) $\dfrac{4}{3} \div \dfrac{2}{5} = \dfrac{\frac{4}{3}}{\frac{2}{5}} = \dfrac{\frac{4}{3} \times ?}{\frac{2}{5} \times ?} = \dfrac{\frac{60}{3}}{?} = \dfrac{?}{?} = ?$;

(g) $\dfrac{2}{7} \div \dfrac{4}{3} = \dfrac{\frac{2}{7}}{\frac{4}{3}} = \dfrac{\frac{2}{7} \times ?}{\frac{4}{3} \times ?} = \dfrac{?}{?} = \dfrac{?}{?} = ?$.

Multiplication and division of fractions

Exercise D

1 (a) $\frac{1}{8} \div \frac{1}{2}$;   (b) $\frac{1}{9} \div \frac{1}{3}$;   (c) $\frac{5}{6} \div \frac{2}{3}$;   (d) $\frac{4}{5} \div \frac{1}{10}$;

   (e) $\frac{1}{2} \div \frac{1}{2}$;   (f) $\frac{5}{8} \div \frac{1}{2}$;   (g) $\frac{5}{9} \div \frac{1}{3}$;   (h) $\frac{3}{4} \div \frac{1}{12}$.

2 (a) $\frac{1}{2} \div \frac{1}{3}$;   (b) $\frac{1}{3} \div \frac{3}{2}$;   (c) $\frac{5}{4} \div \frac{1}{3}$;   (d) $\frac{4}{3} \div \frac{2}{7}$;

   (e) $\frac{3}{7} \div \frac{1}{2}$;   (f) $\frac{4}{5} \div 1\frac{1}{2}$;   (g) $\frac{6}{7} \div 3$;   (h) $2\frac{1}{3} \div \frac{2}{7}$.

Exercise E (Miscellaneous)

1 One class contained 12 girls. The next class had one and one-third times as many girls. How many was that?

2 A plastic container contains two-thirds of a litre. How many times could you fill it from a 10 litre can?

3 How long will it take a boy to eat 20 bars of chocolate if he rations himself to two-thirds of a bar each day?

4 Would you prefer a seventy-second share of £540 or a fiftieth share of £350?

5 A hungry girl eats one quarter of a trifle and then half of what is left. How much trifle does she leave?

6 A quarter of a boy's stamp collection are 'swaps'. Unfortunately, two-thirds of his swaps are torn. What fraction of his collection are untorn stamps?

7 Three-quarters of Janet's record collection are E.P.'s; the rest are L.P.'s. If half of her L.P.'s and all of her E.P.'s are 'pop' records, what fraction of her whole collection do they form?

8 On Monday one-eighth of the pupils in a school were late because of fog. If four-fifths of the latecomers were late again the next day, what fraction of the school arrived on time on Tuesday?

2. Enlargement

1. HOW SHAPES GROW

The patterns in Figure 1 have been made with squares of different sizes. Copy them on squared paper and draw on them any lines which help to show the pattern, like the red lines in Figure 1 (a). What do you notice about each set of pattern lines?

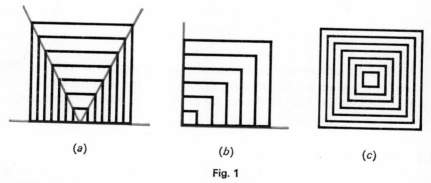

(a)   (b)   (c)

Fig. 1

Investigation 1

Cut out six equilateral triangles of different sizes.

Can you find patterns with pattern lines like those above using your equilateral triangles?

Draw the patterns and also the pattern lines.

23

Investigation 2

Use isometric paper to help you cut out six rhombuses of different sizes, but each having angles as shown in Figure 2.

Using your rhombuses, try to produce patterns like the ones on p. 23.

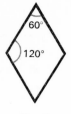

Fig. 2

2. CENTRES OF ENLARGEMENT

In the investigations, did your pattern lines always meet at a point? (They should have done.) This point is called the *centre of enlargement*.

Describe where the centres of enlargement are in Figure 1.

Look at Figure 3, which shows more patterns with pattern lines, and notice how corresponding vertices are always on the same side of the centre of enlargement, *O*. Is this true for each of the patterns in Figure 1?

3. SIMILARITY

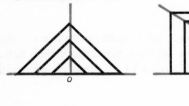
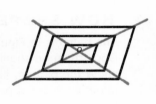

(a)   (b)   (c)

Fig. 3

Each of the patterns in Figure 3 is made with figures which are the same shape. If figures can be arranged to form patterns with pattern lines like this, then we say that the figures are *similar* (they have the same shape).

3.1 The pattern lines

Let us discover what is special about the pattern lines. We have already noted two facts that are true for each set of pattern lines. What are these facts?

In Figure 3 (b), the distances (in cm) from *O* of each corner of the smallest rectangle can be written as an ordered foursome:

$$(0, 0.3, 0.5, 0.4).$$

Write the distances from 0 of the corners of each of the other rectangles in the same way. (Be careful to keep the order the same.)

What do you notice?

How is each ordered foursome related to (0, 0·3, 0·5, 0·4)?

If, instead of choosing the four corners, you chose the four mid-points of the sides, would the same relations be true for each pair of rectangles?

In the same way, write down ordered triples to describe the distances of the vertices from O in Figure 3 (a). Is each ordered triple a multiple of (0·5, 0·5, 0·5)?

Are the triangles in Figure 4 similar? Copy these triangles and draw any straight lines through them which emphasize the pattern.

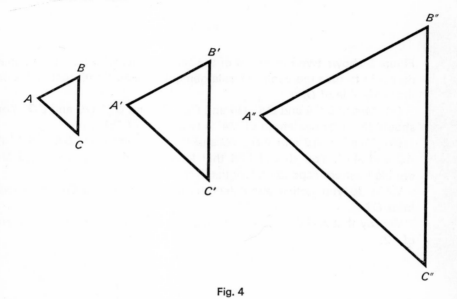

Fig. 4

If you have drawn the pattern lines correctly, you should find that they meet at a single point, O, to the left of triangle ABC,

that
$$OA' = 2OA,$$
$$OB' = 2OB,$$
$$OC' = 2OC,$$

and that
$$OA'' = 4OA,$$
$$OB'' = 4OB,$$
$$OC'' = 4OC.$$

4. SCALE FACTORS

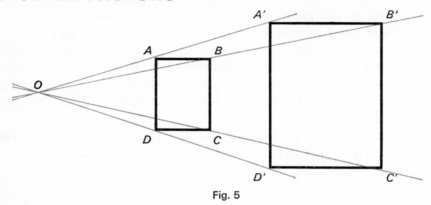

Fig. 5

Figure 5 shows two rectangles of the same shape, with the pattern lines drawn in to give the centre of enlargement at *O* and both rectangles on the same side of *O*.

(*a*) Measure *OA* and *OA'*, *OB* and *OB'*, *OC* and *OC'*, *OD* and *OD'*. You should find that the length of *OA'* is twice that of *OA*, etc.

(*b*) Measure *AB* and *A'B'*, *BC* and *B'C'*, *CD* and *C'D'*, *DA* and *D'A'*, *AC* and *A'C'*. You should find that lengths in the large rectangle are double their corresponding lengths in the small rectangle.

What do you notice about lengths in the rectangles and distances from *O*?

We say that *A'B'C'D'* is an enlargement of *ABCD* with a *scale factor* of $^+2$.

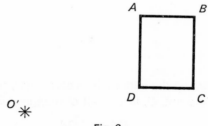

Fig. 6

(*c*) Copy Figure 6, which shows the rectangle *ABCD* of Figure 5 and a point *O'*, onto plain paper. Try to find a method for drawing an enlargement *A'B'C'D'* of *ABCD* using *O'* as the centre of enlargement and a scale factor of $^+2$. (Remember that *A* and *A'* must be on the same side of *O'* and that *O'A* = 2*O'A*.)

Example 1 shows you how to enlarge a shape with scale factor $^+2$.

Example 1

(Follow the instructions for yourselves. Your quadrilateral *need* not be the same as *ABCD* in Figure 7.)

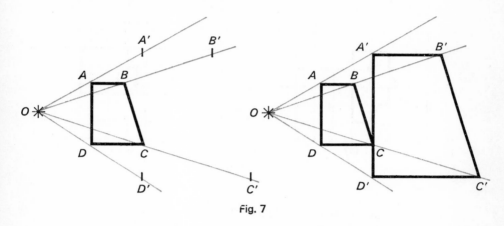

Fig. 7

(i)   Draw a quadrilateral *ABCD* on plain paper and mark a point *O*.

(ii) Draw guide lines from *O* through each point *A*, *B*, *C* and *D*.

(iii) Measure *OA* and mark *A'* on the same side of *O* so that *OA'* is double *OA*. Measure *OB* and mark *B'* on the same side of *O* so that *OB'* is double *OB*. Do the same for *C* and *C'*, and for *D* and *D'*.

(iv) Draw the enlarged figure.

What is the scale factor of the enlargement?

Check your accuracy by measuring *AB* and *A'B'*, *BC* and *B'C'*, etc.

Exercise A

1   Enlarge each of the shapes in Figure 8 with scale factor ⁺2, through the given centre, marked with a star.

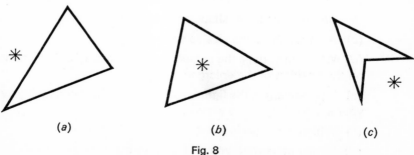

(a)   (b)   (c)

Fig. 8

2 Enlarge each of the shapes in Figure 9 with scale factor ⁺2, through the given centre, marked with a star.

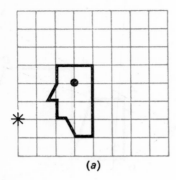

(a)

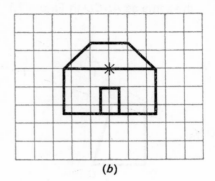

(b)

Fig. 9

3 Enlarge the shape in Figure 10 with scale factor ⁺3, using star 1 as a centre of enlargement.

Do the same for star 2 and star 3 on separate diagrams.

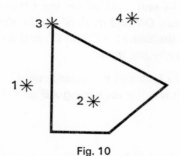

Fig. 10

(a) Are your enlarged figures the same shape as the original?

(b) Are they the same shape as each other?

(c) Are they the same size as each other?

(d) What effect does the position of the centre of enlargement have on the position of the enlarged figure?

(e) If you enlarged the figure, with star 4 as the centre, where would your enlarged figure be drawn?

(f) Which is the easiest one to draw? Why?

(g) Which pattern do you prefer? Why?

4   Mark the following points on squared paper: $A(1, 1)$, $B(4, 1)$, $C(4, 3)$, $D(1, 3)$. Join up the points.

Enlarge *ABCD* with a scale factor of $^+3$ using the origin as centre of enlargement.

On the same diagram enlarge *ABCD* with a scale factor of $^+4$, centre the origin.

What is the relation between the coordinates of the set of vertices of the original figure and each of the enlarged figures?

Is it possible to enlarge *ABCD* with a scale factor of $^+1\frac{1}{2}$, centre the origin?

5   Draw your own shape and enlarge it with a scale factor of $^+3$ and any centre. On the same diagram and with the same centre, enlarge the original shape with a scale factor of $^+1\frac{1}{2}$.

6

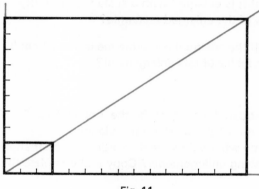

Fig. 11

The rectangles in Figure 11 are similar. What is the scale factor of the enlargement?

Copy Figure 11 and using the pattern lines draw in other rectangles to help you complete the following table.

Length of long side	Length of short side
3	2
	3
6	
9	
$10\frac{1}{2}$	
12	
15	10

If each rectangle you draw is considered as an enlargement of the small rectangle in Figure 11, add a third column to your table, head it 'scale factor' and complete it.

29

Enlargement

7 If you were to enlarge the regular hexagon in Figure 12 with a scale factor of ⁺4, how long would each side of the enlarged hexagon be?

Fig. 12

8 A rectangle measures 2 cm by 3 cm.

(a) If it is enlarged with a scale factor of ⁺$2\frac{1}{2}$, what are the dimensions of the enlarged rectangle?

(b) If the enlarged rectangle measures 12 cm by 18 cm, what is the scale factor of this enlargement?

9 On squared paper, mark the points $O(0, 0)$, $A(^+5, 0)$, $B(0, ^+5)$. Join up the points to form a triangle.
   Onto what points are the vertices of the triangle mapped under the following enlargements? Copy and complete the table.

Enlargement	$O(0, 0)$	$A(^+5, 0)$	$B(0, ^+5)$
(a) From O with scale factor ⁺2			
(b) From O with scale factor ⁺3			
(c) From O with scale factor ⁺$1\frac{1}{2}$			
(d) From A with scale factor ⁺2			
(e) From B with scale factor ⁺3			
(f) From $(^+5, ^+5)$ with scale factor ⁺2			

10 Figure 13 (opposite) shows three shaded figures which have been 'enlarged'. Copy each pair of figures and find the centre of enlargement.

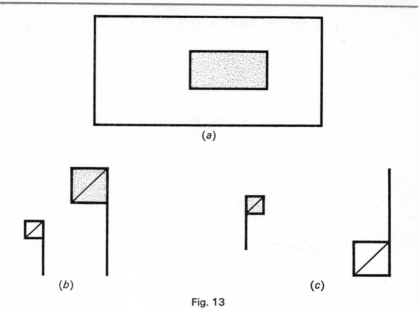

Fig. 13

How do (*b*) and (*c*) differ from the examples you have done so far? What do you think is the scale factor of each 'enlargement'?

4.1 Positive scale factors less than 1

In Figure 13 (*b*) the scale factor of the 'enlargement' from the small flag to the large flag is ⁺2 and lengths are doubled.

If you start with the large flag and obtain the small flag, then all lengths are halved.

We call this an 'enlargement' with scale factor $+\frac{1}{2}$.

Exercise B

1 'Enlarge' each of the shapes in Figure 14 with scale factor $+\frac{1}{2}$.

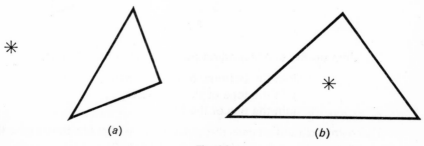

Fig. 14

2 'Enlarge' Figure 15 with a scale factor of $+\frac{1}{3}$.

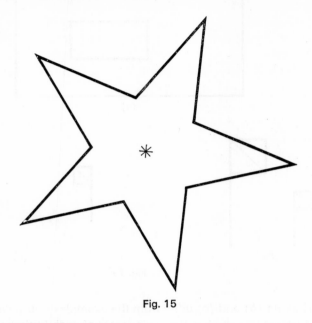

Fig. 15

4.2 Negative scale factors

(*a*) Trace the two flags in Figure 16 onto paper.

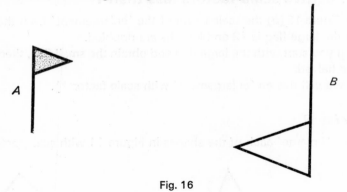

Fig. 16

(*b*) Join up the corresponding points of each flag; that is,

join the bottoms of the flag poles,
join the tops of the flag poles,
join the tips of the flags.

These lines should all pass through a point which is *between* the flags. This is the centre of the 'enlargement'. (Call it *O*.)

(*c*) Measure the distance of the top and bottom of each flag pole and the tip of each flag from *O*. What do you notice?

(*d*) Now measure each flag. You should find that each length on *B* is double its corresponding length on *A*. Also, the flag has been turned upside down.

(*e*) What do you notice about lengths on each flag and distances from *O*?

With distances doubled and the centre of enlargement between the figures, we say that the scale factor of the 'enlargement' of flag *A* is ⁻2; it is a *negative enlargement*.

Example 2 shows you how to enlarge a shape with scale factor ⁻2.

Example 2

(Follow the instructions for yourselves. Your pentagon *need* not be the same as *ABCDE* in Figure 17.)

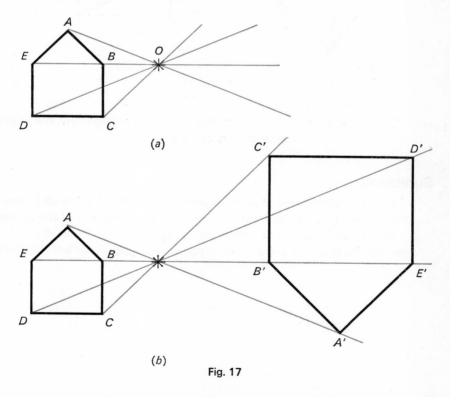

Fig. 17

(i) Draw a pentagon *ABCDE* on plain paper and mark a point *O*.

(ii) Draw guide lines from *A, B, C, D* and *E* through the centre of enlargement, *O*, and extend each one to the other side of *O*.

Enlargement

(iii) Measure *OA* and mark *A'* in line with *O* and *A* but on the opposite side of *O* from *A*. Make *OA'* double the length of *OA*.

(iv) Do the same for *B, C, D* and *E*. Draw the enlarged figure (see Figure 17 (*b*)).

What is the scale factor of the 'enlargement' which maps *A'B'C'D'E'* onto *ABCDE*?

Exercise C

1 Enlarge each of the shapes in Figure 18 with scale factor ⁻2, using the star as centre of enlargement.

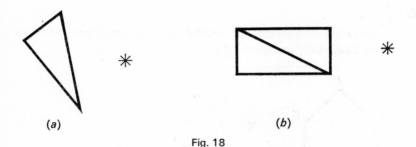

(*a*)   (*b*)

Fig. 18

2 Choose a shape of your own and a centre of enlargement and enlarge this shape with scale factors of ⁻3 and ⁻½.

Summary

(*a*) An enlargement of a figure with scale factor ⁺*k* takes all points of the figure *k* times as far from the centre on the same side of the centre.

(*b*) An enlargement of a figure with scale factor ⁻*k* takes all points of the figure *k* times as far from the centre on the opposite side of the centre.

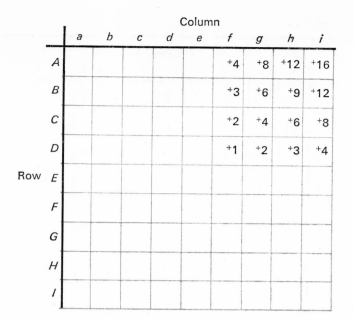

Column

	a	b	c	d	e	f	g	h	i
A						$^+4$	$^+8$	$^+12$	$^+16$
B						$^+3$	$^+6$	$^+9$	$^+12$
C						$^+2$	$^+4$	$^+6$	$^+8$
D						$^+1$	$^+2$	$^+3$	$^+4$
E									
F									
G									
H									
I									

Row

3. Multiplication and division of directed numbers

1. USING NUMBER PATTERNS

In the table above, some of the squares have already been filled with numbers. Let us see if we can make use of number patterns to complete the table in an orderly way.

(a) Copy the table onto squared paper.

(b) Look at column f. Reading from the top downwards, the numbers decrease by $^+1$ each time. Use this fact to complete column f.

(c) Look at column g. Describe the number pattern in your own words and use it to complete column g.

(d) What is happening in columns h and i? Complete these columns.

(e) Look at row E. How should this row be completed?

(f) Describe the number pattern in row D and use it to complete the row.

(g) What is happening in rows C, B and A? Complete these rows.

(h) Complete column e.

You should now have the pattern shown in Figure 1. Check your entries against those in this table and make sure that you understand why we have chosen to fill each of the squares with the particular value shown.

Directed numbers

Column

	a	b	c	d	e	f	g	h	i
A	⁻16	⁻12	⁻8	⁻4	0	⁺4	⁺8	⁺12	⁺16
B	⁻12	⁻9	⁻6	⁻3	0	⁺3	⁺6	⁺9	⁺12
C	⁻8	⁻6	⁻4	⁻2	0	⁺2	⁺4	⁺6	⁺8
D	⁻4	⁻3	⁻2	⁻1	0	⁺1	⁺2	⁺3	⁺4
E	0	0	0	0	0	0	0	0	0
F					0	⁻1	⁻2	⁻3	⁻4
G					0	⁻2	⁻4	⁻6	⁻8
H					0	⁻3	⁻6	⁻9	⁻12
I					0	⁻4	⁻8	⁻12	⁻16

Row

Fig. 1

(*i*) Look carefully at row *F*. Do the numbers increase or decrease as you read from *right* to *left*? Describe the number pattern in your own words and use it to complete the row.

(*j*) Describe the number patterns in rows *G*, *H* and *I* and use them to complete the table.

2. HOW NUMBERS BEHAVE

(*a*) Consider the following statements:

$6 + 4 = 10$;	$^+6 + {}^+4 = {}^+10$;	$^-6 + {}^-4 = {}^-10$;
$12 - 3 = 9$;	$^+12 - {}^+3 = {}^+9$;	$^-12 - {}^-3 = {}^-9$;
$5 > 2$;	$^+5 > {}^+2$;	$^-5 < {}^-2$;
$9 < 11$;	$^+9 < {}^+11$;	$^-9 > {}^-11$.

Those in the left-hand column are about counting numbers, those in the middle column are about positive whole numbers and those in the right-hand column are about negative whole numbers. Check that each of the statements is true.

(*b*) Here are some more statements about counting numbers:

$7 + 8 = 15$;	$20 - 3 = 17$;
$1 < 2$;	$3 + 4 > 5$;
$3 < 6 - 2$;	$4 + 14 = 6 + 12$.

Copy them and in each case write down two similar statements: one about positive whole numbers and one about negative whole numbers.

It is clear that positive whole numbers behave like counting numbers under the operations of addition and subtraction and under the relations 'is greater than' and 'is less than'.

(*c*) Do negative whole numbers behave like counting numbers under the operation of (i) addition, (ii) subtraction?

(*d*) Do negative whole numbers behave like counting numbers under the relation (i) 'is greater than', (ii) 'is less than'?

3. MULTIPLICATION AND DIVISION

3.1 Multiplication

We have seen that positive whole numbers behave exactly like counting numbers under those operations and relations which we have already investigated. Let us suppose that they also behave like counting numbers under the operation of multiplication so that, for example,

$$^+5 \times {}^+3 = {}^+15.$$

3.2 Making tables

(*a*) Figure 2 shows two tables. Table (*a*) is a multiplication table for counting numbers; table (*b*) is a multiplication table for positive whole numbers. Copy and complete these tables.

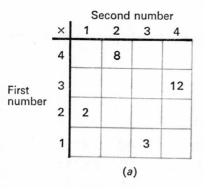

(*a*)

(*b*)

Fig. 2

(*b*) Copy Figure 3 (over page) which shows an incomplete multiplication table for directed whole numbers.

Use your answers to (*a*) to help you fill in the squares coloured red.

Now use number patterns to complete the table. If you have difficulty, look back at Section 1 of this chapter.

What answer do you expect when you multiply a number by 0? How should you label the middle row and the middle column of your table?

What labels should you give to each of the last four rows and to each of the first four columns of your table?

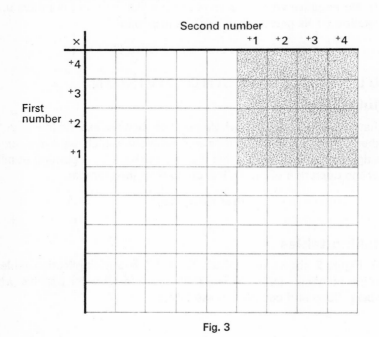

Fig. 3

Keep your completed table; you will need it to help you to answer some of the questions in Exercises *A* and *B*.

Exercise A

1 Use your table to find the values of:

(a)	$^-4 \times {}^+2$;	(b)	$^-3 \times {}^-3$;	(c)	$^+2 \times {}^-3$;
(d)	$^-1 \times {}^-2$;	(e)	$^+1 \times {}^-1$;	(f)	$^-3 \times {}^+1$;
(g)	$^-4 \times {}^+4$;	(h)	$^-4 \times {}^-4$;	(i)	$^+4 \times {}^-4$.

2 The squares coloured red in Figure 3 contain answers to multiplications of one positive whole number by another. What can you say about all the numbers in these red squares?

3 (a) Using a red crayon, colour *all* the squares in your table in which you have written a positive whole number. Describe in your own words the kinds of number which can be multiplied to give an answer in a red shaded square.

(b) Now use a green crayon to shade all the squares in which you have written a negative whole number. Can you say anything about the kinds of number which can be multiplied to give an answer in a green square?

(c) Are there any squares which you have not yet coloured? Which squares are these? Shade them yellow.

(d) Add some more columns to the right of your table and some more rows at the bottom of your table. Decide which colour you should use for each of the new squares that you have added and colour them.

(e) Imagine that more columns are added to the left of your table and more rows at the top of your table. Try to explain how the new squares should be coloured.

(f) In which colour square should you write the answers to:

(i) $^-6 \times {}^+6$;   (ii) $^-2 \times {}^+8$;   (iii) $^+4 \times {}^-10$;   (iv) $^-2 \times {}^-12$?

(g) What do you think are the values of:

(i) $^-6 \times {}^+6$;   (i) $^-2 \times {}^+8$;   (iii) $^+4 \times {}^-10$;   (iv) $^-2 \times {}^-12$?

4 Find the values of:

(a) $^+2 \times {}^-3$;   (b) $^+3 \times {}^-6$;   (c) $^-10 \times {}^+5$;

(d) $^+8 \times {}^+4$;   (e) $^-3 \times 0$;   (f) $^-5 \times {}^-8$;

(g) $0 \times {}^-9$;   (h) $^+6 \times {}^-7$;   (i) $^-4 \times {}^-6$;

(j) $^-6 \times {}^-4$;   (k) $0 \times {}^-27$;   (l) $^-12 \times {}^+3$;

(m) $^-9 \times {}^-7$;   (n) $^-7 \times {}^-9$;   (o) $^+11 \times {}^-6$;

(p) $^+110 \times 0$;   (q) $^+6 \times {}^+8$;   (r) $^-10 \times {}^-10$;

(s) $^+4 \times {}^+4$;   (t) $^-12 \times {}^+12$;   (u) $^-7 \times {}^-8$.

5 Look carefully at your table. What is special about the number $^+1$?

6 Copy the following:

$^+2 \times {}^+4 =$;	$^+2 \times {}^-4 =$;	$^-2 \times {}^+4 =$;	$^-2 \times {}^-4 =$;
$^+2 \times {}^+3\frac{1}{2} =$;	$^+2 \times {}^-3\frac{1}{2} =$;	$^-2 \times {}^+3\frac{1}{2} =$;	$^-2 \times {}^-3\frac{1}{2} =$;
$^+2 \times {}^+3 =$;	$^+2 \times {}^-3 =$;	$^-2 \times {}^+3 =$;	$^-2 \times {}^-3 =$;
$^+2 \times {}^+2\frac{1}{2} =$;	$^+2 \times {}^-2\frac{1}{2} =$;	$^-2 \times {}^+2\frac{1}{2} =$;	$^-2 \times {}^-2\frac{1}{2} =$;
$^+2 \times {}^+2 =$;	$^+2 \times {}^-2 =$;	$^-2 \times {}^+2 =$;	$^-2 \times {}^-2 =$;
$^+2 \times {}^+1\frac{1}{2} =$;	$^+2 \times {}^-1\frac{1}{2} =$;	$^-2 \times {}^+1\frac{1}{2} =$;	$^-2 \times {}^-1\frac{1}{2} =$;
$^+2 \times {}^+1 =$;	$^+2 \times {}^-1 =$;	$^-2 \times {}^+1 =$;	$^-2 \times {}^-1 =$;
$^+2 \times {}^+\frac{1}{2} =$;	$^+2 \times {}^-\frac{1}{2} =$;	$^-2 \times {}^+\frac{1}{2} =$;	$^-2 \times {}^-\frac{1}{2} =$.

First complete the statements written in black and then use number patterns to complete those written in red.

7 Write down the ordered pairs that represent the mapping $x \to {}^+8x$ applied to the set $\{{}^-1, {}^-\frac{1}{2}, 0, {}^+\frac{1}{2}, {}^+1\}$.

8 Write down the ordered pairs that represent the mapping $x \to {}^-3x$ applied to the set $\{{}^-1, {}^-\frac{2}{3}, {}^-\frac{1}{3}, 0, {}^+\frac{1}{3}, {}^+\frac{2}{3}, {}^+1\}$.

9 Suggest sensible values for:

(a) ${}^+1 \times {}^+\frac{1}{4}$;   (b) ${}^+6 \times {}^-\frac{1}{2}$;   (c) ${}^+\frac{1}{4} \times {}^-8$;

(d) ${}^-9 \times {}^-\frac{1}{3}$;   (e) ${}^-\frac{1}{6} \times {}^-10$;   (f) ${}^-\frac{3}{4} \times {}^+\frac{1}{3}$.

10 (a) What are the images under the mapping $x \to x^2$ of the following?

(i) ${}^+5$;   (ii) ${}^+3$;   (iii) ${}^+\frac{1}{2}$;   (iv) ${}^-\frac{1}{2}$;   (v) ${}^-3$;   (vi) ${}^-5$.

(b) What numbers have the following images under the mapping $x \to x^2$?

(i) ${}^+25$;   (ii) ${}^+9$;   (iii) ${}^+4$;   (iv) ${}^+1$.

11 Use your table to solve the equations:

(a) $\square \times {}^+4 = {}^-8$;   (b) $\square \times {}^-1 = {}^+2$;

(c) ${}^+3 \times \square = {}^-12$;   (d) $\square \times {}^-3 = {}^-3$;

(e) ${}^-2 \times \square = 0$;   (f) ${}^-3 \times \square = {}^+9$;

(g) $\square \times {}^-4 = {}^-8$;   (h) $0 \times \square = {}^+4$.

12 Solve the equations:

(a) ${}^-5 \times \square = {}^-20$;   (b) ${}^+6 \times \square = {}^+24$;

(c) $\square \times {}^+4 = {}^-32$;   (d) $\square \times {}^-7 = {}^-28$;

(e) ${}^-2 \times \square = {}^-18$;   (f) ${}^-9 \times \square = 0$;

(g) $\square \times 0 = {}^+10$;   (h) ${}^-6 \times \square = {}^+36$.

3.3 Division

We can use a multiplication table to give answers to division questions in the following way:

Multiplication   Division

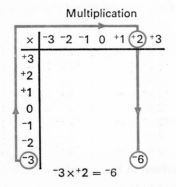 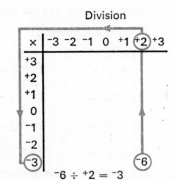

${}^-3 \times {}^+2 = {}^-6$ ${}^-6 \div {}^+2 = {}^-3$

Fig. 4

To find the value of $^-6 \div {}^+2$, we look for the number which multiplied by $^+2$ gives $^-6$.

We find that $^-3 \times {}^+2 = {}^-6$, and we write $^-6 \div {}^+2 = {}^-3$.

Exercise B

1 (*a*) Use your table to solve each equation on the left of the page and so find the value of each expression on the right.

(i)	$\Box \times {}^-3 = {}^-6$;	$^-6 \div {}^-3$;
(ii)	$\Box \times {}^-4 = {}^+16$;	$^+16 \div {}^-4$;
(iii)	$\Box \times {}^+3 = {}^-9$;	$^-9 \div {}^+3$;
(iv)	$\Box \times {}^-4 = {}^-12$;	$^-12 \div {}^-4$;
(v)	$\Box \times {}^+3 = 0$;	$0 \div {}^+3$;
(vi)	$\Box \times {}^+2 = {}^+8$;	$^+8 \div {}^+2$;
(vii)	$\Box \times {}^-2 = {}^-2$;	$^-2 \div {}^-2$;
(viii)	$\Box \times {}^+3 = {}^-3$;	$^-3 \div {}^+3$.

(*b*) What happens when you try to find a value for (i) $^+2 \div 0$, (ii) $^-3 \div 0$?

2 Use the statements:

$$^+4 \times {}^+7 = {}^+28, \quad {}^+4 \times {}^-7 = {}^-28, \quad {}^-4 \times {}^+7 = {}^-28, \quad {}^-4 \times {}^-7 = {}^+28$$

to help you to write down the values of:

(*a*) $^+28 \div {}^+7$;   (*b*) $^-28 \div {}^-7$;   (*c*) $^-28 \div {}^+7$;   (*d*) $^+28 \div {}^-7$.

3 Find the values of:

(*a*) $^+40 \div {}^+10$; (*b*) $^+18 \div {}^+6$;   (*c*) $^+15 \div {}^+5$;   (*d*) $^+24 \div {}^+8$.

Do you think that positive whole numbers behave like counting numbers under the operation of division?

4 Find the values of:

(*a*) $^-12 \div {}^+6$;	(*b*) $^-10 \div {}^-5$;	(*c*) $^+14 \div {}^-7$;
(*d*) $^+5 \div {}^+2$;	(*e*) $^-8 \div {}^+4$;	(*f*) $^-9 \div {}^-2$;
(*g*) $^+27 \div {}^+3$;	(*h*) $^+11 \div {}^-4$;	(*i*) $^-42 \div {}^+6$;
(*j*) $^+33 \div {}^-11$;	(*k*) $^-5 \div {}^-3$;	(*l*) $0 \div {}^+5$;
(*m*) $^-10 \div {}^+4$;	(*n*) $^-9 \div {}^+6$;	(*o*) $^-100 \div {}^+10$.

5 Find the images under the mapping $x \rightarrow {}^+\frac{1}{4}x$ of:

(*a*) $^+6$;   (*b*) $^+3$;   (*c*) 0;   (*d*) $^-3$;   (*e*) $^-6$.

6 Write down the ordered pairs that represent the mapping $x \rightarrow {}^-\frac{1}{5}x$ applied to the set $\{^-5, {}^-3, {}^-1, 0, {}^+1, {}^+3, {}^+5\}$.

3.4 Sensible or silly?

	×	Second number Negative	0	Positive
First number {	Positive	Negative	0	Positive
	0	0	0	0
	Negative	Positive	0	Negative

	÷	Second number Negative	0	Positive
First number {	Positive	Negative	———	Positive
	0	0	———	0
	Negative	Positive	———	Negative

Fig. 5

Positive whole numbers behave like counting numbers under the operations of addition and subtraction and the relations 'is greater than' and 'is less than'. We have supposed that they also behave like counting numbers under the operation of multiplication, and this has led us to think that the tables in Figure 5 are true for *all* directed numbers. In other words, positive numbers (whole, fractional or any measurement of length) behave in the same way as ordinary numbers.

This means that there should be no confusion if we leave out the $^+$ sign. We shall therefore write:

$$3 \quad \text{instead of} \quad {}^+3$$

$$4 \times {}^-\tfrac{1}{4} = {}^-1 \quad \text{instead of} \quad {}^+4 \times {}^-\tfrac{1}{4} = {}^-1;$$

$$^-10 \div 2 = {}^-5 \quad \text{instead of} \quad {}^-10 \div {}^+2 = {}^-5;$$

$$y = 3x + \tfrac{1}{2} \quad \text{instead of} \quad y = {}^+3x + {}^+\tfrac{1}{2};$$

and we shall draw the number line as in Figure 6.

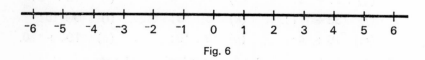

Fig. 6

Having invented rules for the multiplication and division of directed numbers, we shall now investigate whether our rules give sensible results or silly ones.

Investigation 1

(*a*) Do you expect the graph of the relation $y = 2x$ to be a straight line? The ordered pairs (0, 0), (2, 4) and (4, 8) satisfy the relation, and the graph of $y = 2x$ for $0 \leqslant x \leqslant 4$ is drawn in black in Figure 7.

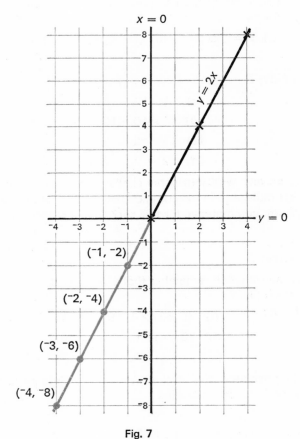

Fig. 7

The straight line, when continued, appears to pass through the points (‾1, ‾2), (‾2, ‾4), (‾3, ‾6) and (‾4, ‾8). Do these ordered pairs also satisfy the relation $y = 2x$?

Does the point (‾2½, ‾5) appear to lie on the red line? Does it satisfy the relation?

Is the red line part of the graph of the relation?

(*b*) Draw the graph of the relation $y = \frac{1}{2}x$ for $0 \leqslant x \leqslant 4$.

Continue the straight line for $^-4 \leqslant x \leqslant 0$. Write down the coordinates of four points which appear to lie on the continuation of the line. Investigate whether these points satisfy the given relation.

Repeat this question for each of the following relations:

(i) $y = \frac{1}{4}x$; (ii) $y = \frac{1}{3}x$; (iii) $y = \frac{3}{2}x$.

(*c*) On separate diagrams, draw the graphs of each of the following relations for $^-4 \leqslant x \leqslant 4$:

(i) $y = ^-2x$; (ii) $y = ^-\frac{1}{2}x$; (iii) $y = ^-\frac{3}{4}x$.

Investigation 2

Work out:

(*a*) $\frac{1}{3} \times 12$, $12 \times \frac{1}{3}$;

(*b*) $^-8 \times 10$, $10 \times ^-8$;

(*c*) $1\frac{1}{2} \times ^-6$, $^-6 \times 1\frac{1}{2}$;

(*d*) $^-2 \times ^-7$, $^-7 \times ^-2$.

Make up and work out some similar examples of your own. Do you think that multiplication is commutative for the set of directed numbers? Is division commutative for this set? Give a reason for your answer.

Investigation 3

(In this investigation remember that you must do the multiplications in the brackets first.)

Work out:

(i) $(5 \times 3) \times 4$, $5 \times (3 \times 4)$;

(ii) $(2 \times 4) \times 6$, $2 \times (4 \times 6)$;

(iii) $(3 \times \frac{1}{2}) \times 7$, $3 \times (\frac{1}{2} \times 7)$.

Does the position of the brackets make any difference to the result?

Now work out the following:

(*a*) $(\frac{1}{2} \times ^-6) \times 7$, $\frac{1}{2} \times (^-6 \times 7)$;

(*b*) $(^-3 \times \frac{1}{3}) \times 6$, $^-3 \times (\frac{1}{3} \times 6)$;

(*c*) $(\frac{1}{2} \times 4) \times ^-\frac{1}{2}$, $\frac{1}{2} \times (4 \times ^-\frac{1}{2})$;

(*d*) $(^-2 \times 6) \times ^-7$, $^-2 \times (6 \times ^-7)$;

(*e*) $(11 \times ^-3) \times ^-4$, $11 \times (^-3 \times ^-4)$;

(*f*) $(^-5 \times ^-10) \times \frac{1}{5}$, $^-5 \times (^-10 \times \frac{1}{5})$;

(*g*) $(^-7 \times ^-10) \times ^-2$, $^-7 \times (^-10 \times ^-2)$.

Does the position of the brackets make any difference to the result when negative numbers are involved?

44

Investigation 4

(*a*)

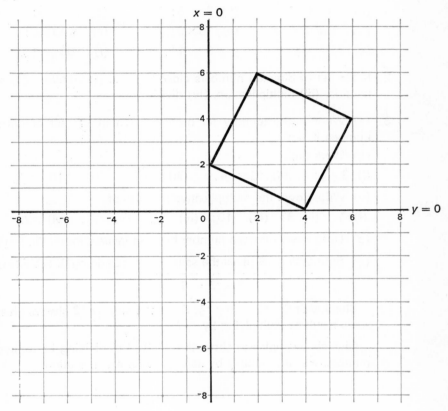

Fig. 8

Draw a square with vertices at (4, 0), (6, 4), (2, 6) and (0, 2). Enlarge the square with centre of enlargement (0, 0) and scale factor $\frac{1}{2}$. Now enlarge the new figure with centre (0, 0) and scale factor ⁻3.

Describe the single transformation which maps the original square onto the final figure. What single scale factor is equivalent to $\frac{1}{2}$× ⁻3? Is this a sensible answer?

(*b*) Repeat (*a*) enlarging first with scale factor ⁻$\frac{1}{2}$ and then with scale factor ⁻3.

(*c*) Repeat (*a*) using a figure and two scale factors of your own choice.

We now see that in all the situations which we have investigated our rules for multiplication and division of directed numbers give the results which we wish them to give.

Directed numbers

Exercise C

1 Find the value of:

 (a) $2 \times {}^-3$;   (b) $3 \times {}^-6$;   (c) ${}^-10 \times 5$;

 (d) ${}^-5 \times {}^-8$;   (e) ${}^-3 \times 9$;   (f) ${}^-123 \times 0$;

 (g) $24 \div {}^-4$;   (h) $0 \div {}^-11$;   (i) ${}^-60 \div {}^-12$.

2 Is the set of directed numbers closed under: (i) addition, (ii) subtraction, (iii) multiplication, (iv) division?

3 (a) What is the identity for multiplication in the set of directed numbers?

(b) Work out:

(i) $3 \times \frac{1}{3}$; (ii) ${}^-\frac{1}{4} \times {}^-4$; (iii) $\frac{1}{7} \times 7$; (iv) ${}^-10 \times {}^-\frac{1}{10}$.

(c) Write down the multiplicative inverses of:

(i) $\frac{1}{3}$; (ii) 3; (iii) ${}^-10$; (iv) ${}^-\frac{1}{10}$; (v) ${}^-\frac{1}{12}$; (vi) ${}^-2$.

(d) Does every directed number have an inverse for multiplication?

(e) Subtracting ${}^-3$ gives the same result as adding 3. For example,

$$8 - {}^-3 = 8 + 3.$$

 Check that $6 \div {}^-2 = 6 \times {}^-\frac{1}{2}$. Does dividing by ${}^-2$ always give the same result as multiplying by ${}^-\frac{1}{2}$?

 Give six examples to show that instead of dividing by a directed number, we can multiply by its inverse for multiplication.

4. Vectors

1. SHOPPING LISTS

When shopping at the supermarket a housewife bought the following groceries:

Tea	$\frac{1}{2}$ kg
Sugar–granulated	2 kg
Sugar–caster	1 kg
Sugar–icing	1 kg
Bacon	$\frac{1}{2}$ kg
Eggs	1 doz.

To save time and effort the housewife decided to use the same list each week and at the end of a month it looked like this:

	Week 1	Week 2	Week 3	Week 4
Tea	$\frac{1}{2}$	$\frac{1}{4}$	$\frac{1}{4}$	
Sugar–granulated	2	4	**1**	1
Sugar–caster	1			$\frac{1}{2}$
Sugar–icing	1	1		$\frac{1}{2}$
Bacon	$\frac{1}{2}$	$\frac{1}{2}$	$\frac{1}{2}$	1
Eggs	1	$1\frac{1}{2}$	2	1

(a) How much caster sugar did she buy in Week 2?

(b) How many eggs did she need in Week 3?

(c) How much icing sugar did she need in Week 4?

(*d*) Could the shopping list for Week 3 be written as follows?

$$\frac{1}{4}$$
$$1$$
$$\frac{1}{2}$$
$$2$$

How might this cause confusion?

(*e*) Could the shopping list for Week 1 be written as follows?

$$\frac{1}{2}$$
$$2$$
$$1$$
$$1$$
$$\frac{1}{2}$$
$$1$$

Would this cause confusion?

(*f*) How much of each item did she buy in the month?

Exercise A

1 A milkman sells gold top, red top and silver top milk. His notebook for Marissal Road looks like this:

	No. 1	No. 2	No. 3	No. 4
Gold	0	2	2	1
Red	2	0	2	3
Silver	1	0	1	2

(*a*) Which house has the most milk?

(*b*) Find the milkman's daily requirements.

(*c*) Find the weekly requirements of each house, assuming the daily orders stay the same.

2 The following table shows the contents of kits for making radio tuners:

	Standard kit	De Luxe kit
Transistors	3	4
Resistors	12	11
Capacitors	10	12
Coils	4	5

(*a*) How many of each item would you need to make both a standard kit and a de luxe kit?

(*b*) Peter and John decide to make a standard radio tuner each, while Jack and David decide to make a de luxe model each. How many of each item would be needed altogether?

3 This table shows the sales of a school tuck shop for one week:

	Monday	Tuesday	Wednesday	Thursday	Friday
Crisps	200	150	173	174	123
Sweets	50	45	40	35	25
Peanuts	25	20	15	20	15
Ice-creams	50	40	75	100	125
Lollies	20	45	80	125	200

(*a*) Find the total sales of each item.

(*b*) Crisps cost 2p, sweets 1p, peanuts 1·5p, ice-creams 2·5p and lollies 1·5p. How much money was taken in the whole week?

(*c*) Can you draw any conclusions about sales at the tuck shop from the information given?

2. SAVING TIME

(*a*) It is tedious to have to write out a table with headings every time. As long as we agree on the order in which the list is going to be written, we need not bother to write out the headings. For example, the housewife's list for Week 2 could be written

$$\begin{pmatrix} \frac{1}{4} \\ 4 \\ 0 \\ 1 \\ \frac{1}{2} \\ 1\frac{1}{2} \end{pmatrix}.$$

Long brackets are often used around sets of numbers like this to show that they belong together.

(i) Write the lists for Weeks 3 and 4 in this way.

(ii) How much did the housewife buy in Weeks 3 and 4 together?

(*b*) A recipe for making 60 Lincoln biscuits involved using the following: $\frac{1}{2}$ kg flour, $\frac{1}{2}$ kg sugar, $\frac{1}{4}$ kg butter, 2 eggs. This could be written

$$\begin{pmatrix} \frac{1}{2} \\ \frac{1}{2} \\ \frac{1}{4} \\ 2 \end{pmatrix}.$$

but we must remember to keep to the same order

flour

sugar

butter

eggs.

If 120 biscuits were needed, the quantities would have to be doubled.

$$2 \times \begin{pmatrix} \frac{1}{2} \\ \frac{1}{2} \\ \frac{1}{4} \\ 2 \end{pmatrix} = \begin{pmatrix} 1 \\ 1 \\ \frac{1}{2} \\ 4 \end{pmatrix}.$$

Copy and complete: $\quad 4 \times \begin{pmatrix} \frac{1}{2} \\ \frac{1}{2} \\ \frac{1}{4} \\ 2 \end{pmatrix} = \begin{pmatrix} \\ \\ \\ \end{pmatrix}.$

How many biscuits would this quantity make?

(c) Sets of numbers which can be added and multiplied in this way are called *vectors*.

In books, letters in bold type like 'a' are usually used for representing vectors. In ordinary handwriting another method is used; a squiggle is put underneath like 'a̰'.

Remember that a letter like 'a' stands for a single number, but a letter like 'a̰' stands for an ordered *set* of numbers, which is a vector.

If $\qquad \mathbf{a} = \begin{pmatrix} \frac{1}{4} \\ 4 \\ 0 \\ 0 \\ \frac{1}{2} \\ 2 \end{pmatrix}$ and $\mathbf{b} = \begin{pmatrix} 0 \\ 1 \\ \frac{1}{2} \\ \frac{1}{2} \\ 1 \\ 1 \end{pmatrix},$

then we write $\qquad \mathbf{a} + \mathbf{b} = \begin{pmatrix} \frac{1}{4} \\ 5 \\ \frac{1}{2} \\ \frac{1}{2} \\ 1\frac{1}{2} \\ 3 \end{pmatrix}.$

What do you think 2a could stand for? What about $\frac{1}{2}$a?

Exercise B

1 A wireless manufacturer needs the following to make up Model *M*: 4 transistors, 3 capacitors, 2 resistors, 4 coils.

(a) Write these requirements as a vector **m**.

(b) How many of each item would be needed for making 5 Model *M*'s?

Give your answer as a vector.

(c) Model *N* requires 5 transistors, 2 capacitors, 3 resistors, 3 coils. Write this as a vector **n**.

(d) Find 5**m** + 3**n**. How many of each type would this make?

2 Susan, Bridget and Jennifer decide to make their own dresses for a party.

Susan's pattern needs $4\frac{1}{2}$ m of velvet, 1 m of nylon, 4 m of binding and 3 buttons.

Bridget's dress and jacket need $1\frac{1}{2}$ m of velvet, 5 m of nylon, $1\frac{1}{2}$ m of binding and no buttons.

Jennifer prefers a shift and needs $2\frac{1}{2}$ m of velvet, 2 m of binding and no buttons.

Write down their requirements as vectors. Add your three vectors to find the total requirements.

3 Five shops hold the following stocks of records:

Shop A has 60 L.P.s, 87 E.P.s, 112 singles;
Shop B has 103 L.P.s, 41 E.P.s, 58 singles;
Shop C only stocks L.P.s and has 72 of them;
Shop D is selling off its stock and has 23 E.P.s and 12 singles left;
Shop E specializes in E.P.s and singles and has 275 records in stock, of which 157 are singles.

Write out the stock of each shop as a vector. Find the total number of each type of record.

4
$$a = \begin{pmatrix} 1 \\ 2 \\ 3 \\ 4 \end{pmatrix}, \quad b = \begin{pmatrix} 3 \\ 4 \\ 5 \\ 6 \end{pmatrix}, \quad c = \begin{pmatrix} 1 \\ 4 \\ 2 \\ 3 \end{pmatrix}.$$

Find:

(a) $3a$;   (b) $\frac{1}{2}b$;   (c) $4c$;

(d) $a+b$;   (e) $b+c$;   (f) $c+a$;

(g) $a+b+c$;   (h) $2(a+b)$;   (i) $2a+2b$.

5 A garage always orders spare parts in the following order:

Pistons
Main bearings
Radiators
Spark plugs
Carburettors.

During one week four cars are being repaired, *A*, *B*, *C* and *D*.

A requires 4 new pistons, 1 main bearing and 4 spark plugs.
B requires 1 carburettor, 1 radiator and 4 spark plugs.
C requires 1 carburettor, 4 spark plugs, 1 radiator and 4 pistons.
D requires 4 pistons, 1 radiator, 4 spark plugs and 1 carburettor.

For the first time the ordering is left to the apprentice and he put in the following order:

$$
\underset{A}{\begin{pmatrix}4\\1\\0\\4\\0\end{pmatrix}} + \underset{B}{\begin{pmatrix}1\\1\\4\\0\\0\end{pmatrix}} + \underset{C}{\begin{pmatrix}4\\0\\1\\4\\1\end{pmatrix}} + \underset{D}{\begin{pmatrix}4\\0\\1\\4\\1\end{pmatrix}} = \overset{\text{Total}}{\begin{pmatrix}13\\2\\6\\12\\2\end{pmatrix}}.
$$

Is this correct? If not, put it right.

3. JOURNEYS

(*a*) Look at Figure 1. The ship has moved from the port, *P*, to the position *S*. How would you describe the position of the ship relative to the port?

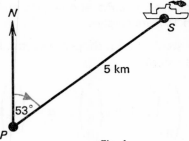

Fig. 1

(*b*) Figure 2 shows the same port and ship drawn on a grid. How would you describe the position of the ship in this case?

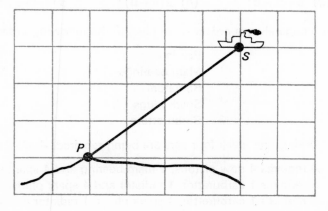

Fig. 2

Instead of saying 4 km east and 3 km north we could write

$$\binom{4}{3}.$$

Notice that the distance east is written first. It could be the other way round, but whichever way we write it we must stick to it so as to avoid confusion.

Suppose the ship moves from position, *S*, and its movement is $\binom{2}{6}$.

Its position then relative to the port is given by

$$\binom{4}{3} + \binom{2}{6} = \binom{6}{9}.$$

These sets of numbers describing positions are also *vectors*.

If, from the position shown, the ship moved $\binom{-2}{3}$, this would be a move of two squares to the *west* and three squares *north*. The position from the port after the move would be given by

$$\binom{4}{3} + \binom{-2}{3} = \binom{2}{6}.$$

If the ship now moved $\binom{-2}{-6}$, where would it be?

Exercise C

1 Write down the journeys from *A* to *B*, *C* to *D*, *E* to *F* and *G* to *H* in Figure 3 as vectors.

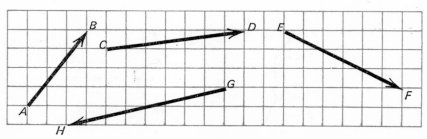

Fig. 3

2 (*a*) The first stage of the journey from Fish Port to Jacob's Creek can be written $\binom{3}{0}$. The second stage is $\binom{0}{2}$. Write the other stages in this way.

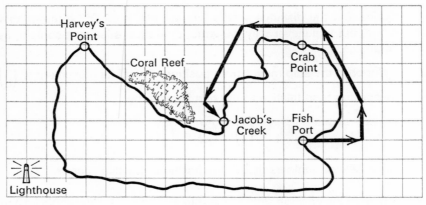

Fig. 4

(*b*) Add up the 6 vectors for the stages. Can you see a method for checking your answer?

(*c*) Write down some vectors for a journey from Fish Port to Harvey's Point via the Lighthouse.

(*d*) Give your partner a starting point and some vectors, and ask him for the destinations.

3 The moves in a game of chess can be described using vectors.

If you have never played chess, learn the basic moves and play with your partner.

If you have played chess, think about the moves in terms of vectors.

Figure 5 shows some moves of a knight. They are

$$\binom{2}{1}, \quad \binom{1}{2}, \quad \binom{-2}{1}, \quad \binom{1}{2}.$$

Give the vectors for some more knight's moves.

Knight

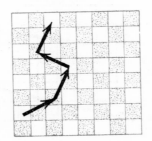

Fig. 5

In the course of a game, a queen makes the following pairs of moves:

(a) $\begin{pmatrix} 3 \\ 0 \end{pmatrix}$, $\begin{pmatrix} 0 \\ 3 \end{pmatrix}$; (b) $\begin{pmatrix} 2 \\ 2 \end{pmatrix}$, $\begin{pmatrix} -4 \\ 0 \end{pmatrix}$;

(c) $\begin{pmatrix} 0 \\ -4 \end{pmatrix}$, $\begin{pmatrix} 4 \\ 4 \end{pmatrix}$; (d) $\begin{pmatrix} 6 \\ 0 \end{pmatrix}$, $\begin{pmatrix} -3 \\ 3 \end{pmatrix}$.

In each of the four cases she could have made the move in one if there had been no other pieces in her way. What single moves could she have made?

Would it make any difference if the order of the single moves was reversed?

4 Use vectors to describe a chess problem and see if your partner can solve it.

5 If **a** and **b** are two vectors, is **a** + **b** the same as **b** + **a**?

6 *Snakes and Ladders*

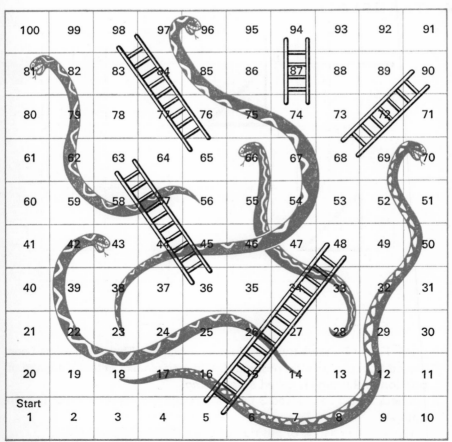

Fig. 6

(*a*) Give the column vectors for each *snake* and each *ladder*.

(*b*) (i) If you land on square 96, where do you finish up? What is this move as a vector?

(ii) If you land on square 36, then throw a 3, where do you finish up? Represent each of these three moves as column vectors. What is the overall move as a vector?

(iii) If you land on square 74, and then throw a 2, where do you finish up? Describe this series of moves by using vectors.

(*c*) (i) What combination of scores will get you to the end in the shortest possible number of throws?

(ii) Now give your answer as a series of vectors.

(*d*) Play the game of Snakes and Ladders with your neighbour. Keep a record of the moves using vectors.

4. TRANSLATIONS

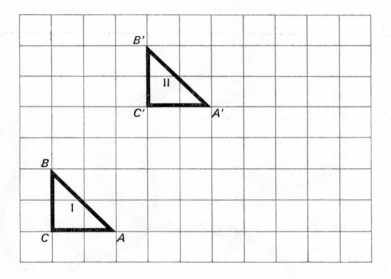

Fig. 7

(*a*) Figure 7 shows two positions of a triangle. The triangle has been moved from position I to position II. You may remember that a change of position of this type is called a *translation*.

Check that *A* has moved 3 units along and 4 units up in order to map onto *A'*.

What is the change of position of point *B*? And of point *C*?

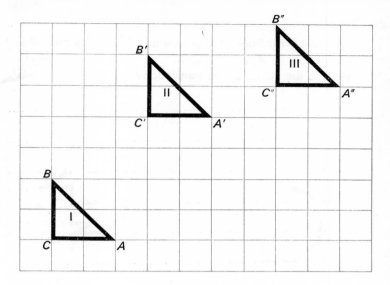

Fig. 8

(*b*) The triangle is now translated from position II to position III (see Figure 8). How far has *A'* moved along and how far up?
Have *B'* and *C'* moved the same amount?

(*c*) Describe the overall change of position from I to III.

(*d*) As with shopping lists and journeys we can again use vectors. The change of position of every point of the triangle can be described by the same vector. This is the vector of the translation.

The vector of the translation from I to II is $\begin{pmatrix} 3 \\ 4 \end{pmatrix}$,

the vector of the translation from II to III is $\begin{pmatrix} 4 \\ 1 \end{pmatrix}$,

and the vector of the combined translation from I to III is

$$\begin{pmatrix} 3 \\ 4 \end{pmatrix} + \begin{pmatrix} 4 \\ 1 \end{pmatrix} = \begin{pmatrix} 7 \\ 5 \end{pmatrix}.$$

Exercise D

1 In Figure 9 Mr Poly undergoes a translation. Describe the change of position of (i) *A*, (ii) *B*, (iii) *C*.
What is the vector of the translation?

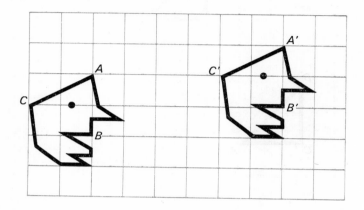

Fig. 9

2 Figure 10 shows three positions of an iron. Write down the vectors of the following translations:

(*a*) I to II; (*b*) II to III; (*c*) I to III.

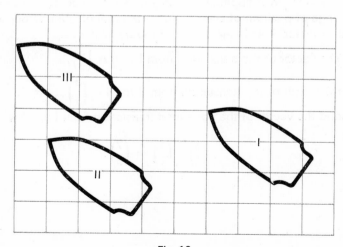

Fig. 10

3   A translation has vector $\begin{pmatrix} 1 \\ 2 \end{pmatrix}$. Onto what points would the translation map the following points?

    (*a*) (2, 3);   (*b*) (1, ⁻2);   (*c*) (⁻1, ⁻2).

4   What translation would map (3, 4) onto (6, 2)? Onto what point would the translation map (1, ⁻1)?

5   Find what point would map onto (2, 3) after a translation with vector $\begin{pmatrix} 5 \\ 6 \end{pmatrix}$.

6   The point (2, 3) is mapped onto the point (⁻1, 2) via the point (2, ⁻2), by two translations.

    (*a*) What are the vectors of the two translations?
    (*b*) What is the vector of the combined translation?

7   Mark the points: *A*(2, 6), *B*(6, 5), *C*(5, 2), *D*(3, 3), *E*(5, 7) on squared paper.

    (*a*) Write down the vectors of the translations such that
    (i) *A* → *B*,   (ii) *B* → *C*,   (iii) *C* → *D*,   (iv) *D* → *E*.
    (*b*) Write down the vector of the translation *A* → *E*.
    (*c*) What is the connection between the vectors in (*a*) and (*b*)?

Interlude

MATHEMATICAL EMBROIDERY

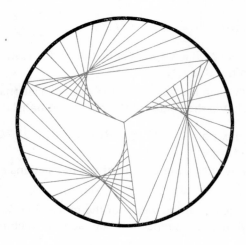

Fig. 1

Equipment: thin cardboard, coloured thread or wool, thick needle, com-passes, protractor, ruler.

Pattern 1

On your cardboard draw a circle of radius 6 cm, prick 24 holes at equal distances round it. Number them 0–23. Thread your needle with a long piece of thread or wool and tie a knot in one end. Now join:

0 to 6, 1 to 7, 2 to 8, 3 to 9, ... 17 to 23, 18 to 0, 19 to 1 ... 22 to 4, 23 to 5 (see Figure 2). The dotted lines show the thread on the under side of the pattern.

Figure 3 shows how the same pattern can be made by using less thread, while Figure 4 shows the finished result. We say that the line segments (threads) *envelop* a circle.

60

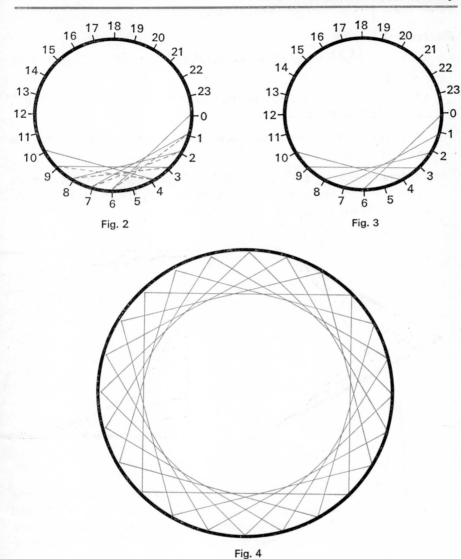

Fig. 2

Fig. 3

Fig. 4

Patterns 2 and 3

What would happen if you joined

(a) 0 to 3, 1 to 4, 2 to 5, ... 20 to 23, 21 to 0, 22 to 1, 23 to 2; or

(b) 0 to 9, 1 to 10, 2 to 11, ... 14 to 23, 15 to 0, 16 to 1, ...?

Using circles of the same radius, try for yourself and see. Explain what would happen if you joined

0 to 12, 1 to 13, 2 to 14 ....

Pattern 4

Mark 36 points at equal distances round a circle and label them 0 to 35. Join:

1 to 2, 2 to 4, 3 to 6, 4 to 8, 5 to 10 ... 17 to 34, 18 to 0, 19 to 2, 20 to 4, ... 33 to 30, 34 to 32, 35 to 34.

What curve do the line segments envelop this time? Find out what it is called and why.

It is not necessary to start with circles. Figures 5 and 6 show two more ideas. You may like to try these for yourself and perhaps the more complicated pattern in Figure 1.

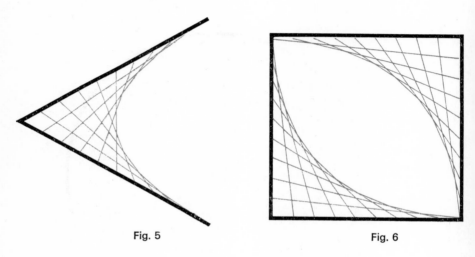

Fig. 5   Fig. 6

It is possible to produce many attractive designs by joining holes to one another in differently ordered ways and using a selection of coloured threads. Remember that the holes must be equally spaced apart and that, generally speaking, the closer they are together the better the results. Now try to make some designs of your own.

If you prefer, you can, of course, produce the patterns by drawing.

5. Punctuation and Order

In this chapter we shall look at ways in which members or elements of sets can be combined by operations.

Examples of operations which we have already met are addition, subtraction, multiplication, division and intersection. The first four are operations for combining numbers and the fifth for combining sets.

1. ORDER OF OPERATIONS

1.1 Does order matter?

(a) By performing first the red operation and then the black operation, find the value of

$$12 \div 6 \div 2.$$

Now find the value, performing first the black and then the red operation. Do you get the same answer as before?

$12 \div 6 \div 2$ could mean either 'divide 12 by 6 and then divide the result by 2' or 'divide 6 by 2 and then divide 12 by the result'. We do not know which division to work out first!

Since the meaning is not clear, we need punctuation to help us. So we use a bracket to show that *whatever is inside the bracket must be worked out first.*

Thus $(12 \div 6) \div 2 = 2 \div 2 = 1,$

and $12 \div (6 \div 2) = 12 \div 3 = 4.$

(*b*) Now work out:

$$
\begin{array}{lll}
\text{(i)} & (13+8)+3, & 13+(8+3); \\
\text{(ii)} & (15+4)+7, & 15+(4+7); \\
\text{(iii)} & (11+9)+5, & 11+(9+5); \\
\text{(iv)} & (23+31)+14, & 23+(31+14).
\end{array}
$$

Comment on your answers.

Each of the expressions in (*b*) contains only one type of operation, the operation of addition. Whatever numbers we use, the brackets make no difference to the result, and we say that the operation of addition is *associative*.

Since $(13+8)+3 = 13+(8+3)$, there is no confusion if we omit the brackets and write $$13+8+3.$$

(*c*) Is there confusion if we write $12 \div 6 \div 2$?
Is the operation of division associative?

Exercise A

1 Work out:

(*a*) $(12-7)-4$, $12-(7-4)$;
(*b*) $(15-6)-5$, $15-(6-5)$;
(*c*) $(10-8)-1$, $10-(8-1)$;
(*d*) $(23-11)-4$, $23-(11-4)$.

Is the operation of subtraction associative? Do you need to try other triples of numbers in order to be sure?

2 Work out:

(*a*) $(7\times5)\times4$, $7\times(5\times4)$;
(*b*) $(2\times6)\times5$, $2\times(6\times5)$;
(*c*) $(10\times7)\times2$, $10\times(7\times2)$;
(*d*) $(3\times11)\times8$, $3\times(11\times8)$.

Is the operation of multiplication associative? Do you need to try other triples of numbers in order to be sure?

3 If
$$A = \{2, 4, 6, 8, 10, 12\},$$
$$B = \{1, 2, 3, 4, 5, 6, 7, 8\},$$
$$C = \{6, 7, 8, 9, 10, 11\},$$

list the members of the sets $A \cap B$ and $B \cap C$.
Find $(A \cap B) \cap C$ and $A \cap (B \cap C)$. Are they equal?

Copy Figure 1 and 'post' each of the numbers 1, 2, 3, 4, 5, 6, 7, 8, 9, 10, 11 and 12 in the correct region. The numbers 1 and 2 have been 'posted' for you.

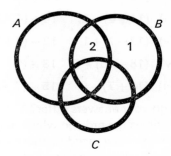

Fig. 1

4   If M = {multiples of 3 that are less than 40},

N = {odd numbers that are less than 50},

S = {square numbers that are less than 60},

list the members of the sets $M \cap N$ and $N \cap S$.
Is $(M \cap N) \cap S = M \cap (N \cap S)$?
Do you think that the operation of intersection is associative?

5   Make up three sets of numbers P, Q, R.
Find $(P \cap Q) \cap R$ and $P \cap (Q \cap R)$.
Is there confusion if you write $P \cap Q \cap R$?

6   Suppose 12 A 20 means 'take the average of 12 and 20'. Then 12 A 20 = 16. What is 20 A 24?
Work out: (*a*) (12 A 20) A 24; (*b*) 12 A (20 A 24). Is the operation A associative? Do you need to try other triples of numbers in order to be sure?

1.2   + and −

(*a*) Is $(13+8)+3$ equal to $13+(8+3)$? Is there any confusion if we write $13+8+3$?
(*b*) Is $(12-7)-4$ equal to $12-(7-4)$? Is there any confusion if we write $12-7-4$?

So far, we have worked out expressions which contain only one type of operation. We shall now investigate whether punctuation is needed when an expression contains both + and −.

65

(*c*) Work out the following pairs of expressions:

$\quad$ (i) $\quad (15+6)-3, \quad 15+(6-3)$;

$\quad$ (ii) $\quad (20-11)+5, \quad 20-(11+5)$;

$\quad$ (iii) $\quad (14+4)-2, \quad 14+(4-2)$;

$\quad$ (iv) $\quad (12-7)+1, \quad 12-(7+1)$;

$\quad$ (v) $\quad (18-10)+5, \quad 18-(10+5)$;

$\quad$ (vi) $\quad (15+7)-6, \quad 15+(7-6)$.

For which pairs do your answers differ?

We see that sometimes the order in which the operations are performed does matter, and therefore we need to know which operation to do first. We usually show this by using brackets. But in expressions which contain only $+$ and $-$, we omit brackets when the order in which the operations are to be performed is the same as the order in which they are written.

Thus we write $12-7-4$ instead of $(12-7)-4$, and so

$$12-7-4 = 5-4 = 1.$$

(*d*) Work out:

$\quad$ (i) $\quad 16-2-1$;

$\quad$ (ii) $\quad 14-5+2$;

$\quad$ (iii) $\quad 11+2-8$;

$\quad$ (iv) $\quad 20-12+3-7$;

$\quad$ (v) $\quad 15-1-2-3$.

Exercise B

Work out each of the following expressions. *If there are no brackets, then the operations should be done in the order in which they are written.*

1	$17-5-6$.	2	$13-7+2$.
3	$16+4-9$.	4	$4+3-7$.
5	$20-(3+8)$.	6	$20-3+8$.
7	$15+4+1$.	8	$16-6-8$.
9	$18-5-3$.	10	$18-(5+3)$.
11	$18-5+3$.	12	$11-(4-1)$.
13	$7+2-3-4$.	14	$12-3-2-7$.
15	$30-(5+4+9)$.	16	$4-3-1+11$.

17 $100-(20+30+40)$.   18 $15-12+7-1$.

19 $46-6+10+2$.   20 $46-(6+10+2)$.

1.3 Using punctuation

(*a*) Work out the following pairs of expressions:

(i)	$(5\times 4)+7$,	$5\times (4+7)$;
(ii)	$(6\times 11)-3$,	$6\times (11-3)$;
(iii)	$(18\div 2)+4$,	$18\div (2+4)$;
(iv)	$(24\div 6)-3$,	$24\div (6-3)$;
(v)	$(7+3)\times 5$,	$7+(3\times 5)$;
(vi)	$(8-2)\times 3$,	$8-(2\times 3)$;
(vii)	$(4+8)\div 2$,	$4+(8\div 2)$;
(viii)	$(12-9)\div 3$,	$12-(9\div 3)$;
(ix)	$(5\times 6)\div 3$,	$5\times (6\div 3)$;
(x)	$(12\div 3)\times 2$,	$12\div (3\times 2)$.

For which pairs do your answers differ?
Is punctuation usually necessary?

(*b*) Make up six more pairs of expressions like those in (*a*), and work them out.

Exercise C

Copy the following statements and put in brackets to make the statements true.

1 $3\times 5+7 = 36$.   2 $3\times 5+7 = 22$.

3 $1+4\times 8 = 40$.   4 $1+4\times 8 = 33$.

5 $6-2\times 2 = 2$.   6 $6-2\times 2 = 8$.

7 $11+9\times 3 = 38$.   8 $11+9\times 3 = 60$.

9 $15-2\times 7 = 1$.   10 $16\div 4+4 = 2$.

11 $18-6\div 3 = 4$.   12 $17-7+1 = 9$.

13 $5-3-2 = 0$.   14 $20\div 2\times 5 = 50$.

15 $14+8\div 2 = 11$.   16 $16-2\times 6 = 4$.

1.4 Letters for numbers

We have seen that when we have to do more than one operation we nearly always need to know which to do first, since, for example,

$$(3 \times 5) + 4 \quad \text{is not equal to} \quad 3 \times (5 + 4).$$

Similarly, if a stands for any number,

$$(3 \times a) + 4 \quad \text{is not equal to} \quad 3 \times (a + 4).$$

We already know that $3 \times a$ is written as $3a$. We shall therefore write:

$$(3 \times a) + 4 \quad \text{as} \quad (3a) + 4 \quad \text{or more simply as} \quad 3a + 4$$

and $\qquad\qquad\qquad 3 \times (a + 4) \quad \text{as} \quad 3(a + 4).$

Brackets are thought to be unnecessary in the expression $(3a) + 4$ since the closeness of the 3 and the a suggests that the multiplication should be done first.

(*a*) Find the value of $3a + 4$ when (i) $a = 2$, (ii) $a = 0$, (iii) $a = 7$.

(*b*) Find the value of $3(a + 4)$ when (i) $a = 2$, (ii) $a = 0$, (iii) $a = 7$.

(*c*) We write $3 \times a$ as $3a$. Can we write 3×5 as 35?

(*d*) What is meant by (i) $5c$, (ii) bc?

(*e*) The expression $2b - 5$ means 'multiply 2 by b and then subtract 5 from the result'. What do you think is meant by the expression $2(b - 5)$? Find the value of each of these expressions when

$$\text{(i)} \quad b = 6, \qquad \text{(ii)} \quad b = 10, \qquad \text{(iii)} \quad b = 14.$$

(*f*) The expression $\frac{c}{3} + d$ means 'divide c by 3 and then add d to the result'. What do you think is meant by the expression $\frac{c}{3 + d}$? Find the value of each of these expressions when $c = 15$ and $d = 2$.

(*g*) Write in words what you think is meant by each of the following expressions:

$$\text{(i)} \quad \frac{a}{b} + c, \qquad \text{(ii)} \quad \frac{a}{b + c}, \qquad \text{(iii)} \quad \frac{a - b}{c}, \qquad \text{(iv)} \quad a - \frac{b}{c}.$$

Find the value of each of these expressions when $a = 12$, $b = 4$ and $c = 2$.

(*h*) If an expression contains only $+$ and $-$ and has no brackets, in what order should you do the operations?

If $a = 5$, $b = 2$ and $c = 7$, find the value of

$$\text{(i)} \quad a - b + c, \qquad \text{(ii)} \quad 3a - b - c, \qquad \text{(iii)} \quad 8a - 5b + 3c.$$

(*i*) If $a = 8$, find the value of:

$\qquad$ (i) $a+a+a,$ $\qquad$ (ii) $3a.$

Explain why your answers are equal.

(*j*) If $b = 3$, find the value of:

$\qquad$ (i) $4b;$ $\qquad\qquad$ (ii) $b+3b;$ $\qquad\qquad$ (iii) $b+b+b+b;$

$\qquad$ (iv) $5b-b;$ $\qquad\quad$ (v) $8b-b-3b;$ $\qquad$ (vi) $2b-b+3b.$

What do you notice?

(*k*) What can you say about each of the following expressions?

$\qquad$ (i) $a+4a;$ $\qquad\qquad$ (ii) $a+3a+a;$ $\qquad$ (iii) $4a-a+2a;$

$\qquad$ (iv) $5a;$ $\qquad\qquad\quad$ (v) $8a-a-2a;$ $\qquad$ (vi) $7a-a+4a-5a.$

Which is the simplest of these expressions?

(*l*) Write in shorter form:

$\qquad$ (i) $5b+2b;$ $\qquad\quad$ (ii) $7a-6a;$ $\qquad\qquad$ (iii) $c+3c+2c;$

$\qquad$ (iv) $6x-2x+x;$ $\qquad$ (v) $y-y+2y;$ $\qquad\quad$ (vi) $8d-2d-6d.$

Exercise D

1 If $a = 5$, find the value of:

$\qquad$ (*a*) $4a;$ $\qquad\qquad$ (*b*) $a+2;$ $\qquad\qquad$ (*c*) $2a-6;$

$\qquad$ (*d*) $3a+7;$ $\qquad\quad$ (*e*) $2(a+1);$ $\qquad\quad$ (*f*) $3(4a-19).$

2 If $b = 8$, find the value of:

$\qquad$ (*a*) $5b;$ $\qquad\qquad$ (*b*) $b-4;$ $\qquad\qquad$ (*c*) $3b+3;$

$\qquad$ (*d*) $2b-9;$ $\qquad\quad$ (*e*) $6(b-3);$ $\qquad\quad$ (*f*) $\frac{1}{2}(b+2).$

3 If $a = 4$ and $b = 1$, find the value of:

$\qquad$ (*a*) $5a+b;$ $\qquad\qquad$ (*b*) $5(a+b);$ $\qquad\qquad$ (*c*) $a+5b.$

4 If $a = 10$ and $b = 3$, find the value of:

$\qquad$ (*a*) $2a-3b;$ $\qquad\qquad$ (*b*) $2(a-3b);$ $\qquad\qquad$ (*c*) $3(2a-b).$

5 If $a = 2$ and $b = 7$, find the value of:

$\qquad$ (*a*) $\frac{1}{2}a+b;$ $\qquad\qquad$ (*b*) $\frac{1}{2}(a+b);$ $\qquad\qquad$ (*c*) $a+\frac{1}{2}b;$

$\qquad$ (*d*) $\frac{1}{2}a+\frac{1}{2}b;$ $\qquad\qquad$ (*e*) $\frac{a}{2}+b;$ $\qquad\qquad$ (*f*) $\frac{a+b}{2}.$

6 If $a = 12$ and $b = 6$, find the value of:

(a) $3a - b$; (b) $3(a - b)$; (c) $a(b + 3)$;

(d) $ab + 3$; (e) $a - 2b$; (f) $ab - 2$.

7 If $a = 20$, $b = 5$ and $c = 2$, find the value of:

(a) $ab - c$; (b) $a(b - c)$; (c) $(a - b)c$;

(d) $a - bc$; (e) $\dfrac{a}{b} - c$; (f) $a + b + c$;

(g) $\dfrac{a}{b - c}$; (h) $a - b - c$; (i) $\dfrac{a - b}{c}$;

(j) $a - \dfrac{b}{c}$; (k) $a - (b - c)$; (l) $\dfrac{ac}{b}$.

8 If $a = 3$ and $b = 5$, find the value of:

(a) $a + 2b + 1$; (b) $5a - (b + 4)$; (c) $2a - b + 7$.

9 Write in shorter form:

(a) $x + x + x$; (b) $5y - y - 2y$;

(c) $2a + 3a - 5a$; (d) $b + 7b - 4b$;

(e) $6p - 3p - 2p$; (f) $2q + q + 7q$;

(g) $2c - c + 8c$; (h) $5e - (2e + e)$;

(i) $3x + 2x + 6x + 9x$; (j) $4y + 8y - 3y + y$;

(k) $15a - (3a + a + 6a)$; (l) $9b - 2b + b - 5b$.

2. ORDER OF MAPPINGS

(a) Choose a number. Add 2 and then add 5.

Start with the same number as before, but this time first add 5 and then add 2. What happens?

Fig. 2

Suppose we start with 1. Figure 2 shows that if we add 2 and then add 5, we end with 8. If we add 5 and then add 2, we again end with 8 as shown in Figure 3.

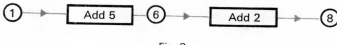

Fig. 3

It seems that the mapping 'add 2 and then add 5' is the same (that is has the same effect) as the mapping 'add 5 and then add 2'. By starting with several other numbers, try to decide whether this statement is true.

(*b*)

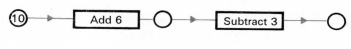

Fig. 4

The flow diagram in Figure 4 shows the mapping 'add six and then subtract 3'. If you start with 10, what number do you end with?

What mapping does the flow diagram in Figure 5 show? If you start with 10, do you end with the same number as you did in Figure 4?

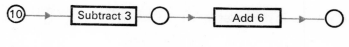

Fig. 5

Try starting with other numbers. If you start with the same number in both flow diagrams, do you always end with the same number?

Is the mapping 'add 6 and then subtract 3' the same as 'subtract 3 and then add 6'?

(*c*) Draw a pair of flow diagrams like those in Figures 4 and 5 to show the mappings 'subtract 2 and then subtract 1' and 'subtract 1 and then subtract 2'.

If you start with the same number in both diagrams do you always end with the same number?

Is the mapping 'subtract 2 and then subtract 1' the same as the mapping 'subtract 1 and then subtract 2'?

Is the relation $x \rightarrow x - 2 - 1$ the same relation as $x \rightarrow x - 1 - 2$?

(*d*) Do you think that:

(i) 'add *a* and then add *b*' is the same as 'add *b* and then add *a*';

(ii) 'add *a* and then subtract *b*' is the same as 'subtract *b* and then add *a*';

(iii) 'subtract *a* and then subtract *b*' is the same as 'subtract *b* and then subtract *a*'?

When numbers are combined by only + and −, we can change the order of the numbers and the operations associated with them. For example:
$$4+6-3 = 4-3+6,$$
and
$$5-2-1 = 5-1-2.$$

We can sometimes use this fact to find a quick method for computing. For example:
$$107+79-7 = 107-7+79 = 100+79 = 179.$$

We can also use it to write expressions more simply. For example:
$$a+3+a = a+a+3 = 2a+3.$$

(*e*) Use short methods to find the values of:

(i) $79+38+21$;

(ii) $167+289-67$;

(iii) $37-19+63-11$.

(*f*) Write in a simpler form:

(i) $7+a+8$;

(ii) $5b-2-b$;

(iii) $3x+y+5x$.

(*g*)

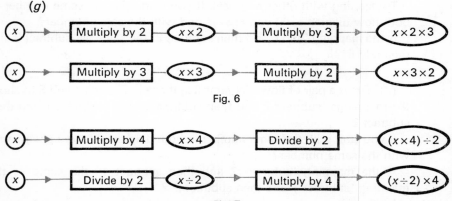

Fig. 6

Fig. 7

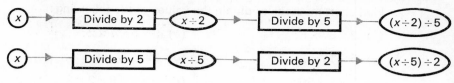

Fig. 8

By starting with several different numbers in each of the pairs of flow diagrams in Figures 6, 7 and 8, try to decide whether

(i) 'multiply by 2 and then multiply by 3' is the same as 'multiply by 3 and then multiply by 2';

(ii) 'multiply by 4 and then divide by 2' is the same as 'divide by 2 and then multiply by 4';

(iii) 'divide by 2 and then divide by 5' is the same as 'divide by 5 and then divide by 2'.

When numbers are combined by only $\times$ and $\div$, we can change the order of the numbers and the operations associated with them. For example:

$$25 \times 19 \times 4 = 25 \times 4 \times 19,$$

and

$$(12 \times 17) \div 2 = (12 \div 2) \times 17.$$

(*h*) Use this fact to help you to find the value of:

(i) $25 \times 19 \times 4$;

(ii) $(12 \times 17) \div 2$.

(*i*) Now use it to write these expressions in a simpler form:

(i) $7 \times a \times 5$;

(ii) $(18 \times b) \div 2$.

Exercise E

1 Find short methods to obtain the values of the following:

(*a*) $99 + 38 + 1$;

(*b*) $6 + 17 + 34 + 3$;

(*c*) $35 + 87 + 65$;

(*d*) $23 + 18 - 3$;

(*e*) $980 + 157 + 20$;

(*f*) $144 + 194 - 44$;

(*g*) $25 + 72 + 28 + 75$;

(*h*) $15 + 29 - 5 + 11$;

(*i*) $993 + 672 + 7$;

(*j*) $19 - 12 + 15 - 8 + 11 + 5$;

(*k*) $29 - 17 - 9 + 27$;

(*l*) $53 + 81 + 47 + 44 + 19 + 56$;

(*m*) $26 - 8 + 18 - 16$;

(*n*) $49 + 59 - 19 - 9$.

2   Find short methods to obtain the values of the following:

(a) $2 \times 37 \times 5$;

(b) $9 \times 5 \times 7 \times 2$;

(c) $5 \times 11 \times 3 \times 2$;

(d) $25 \times 37 \times 4$;

(e) $2 \times 9 \times 50$;

(f) $5 \times 5 \times 5 \times 2 \times 2 \times 2$;

(g) $4 \times 8 \times 7 \times 25$;

(h) $\frac{1}{3} \times 17 \times 12$;

(i) $\frac{1}{2} \times 51 \times 20$;

(j) $\frac{1}{5} \times 16 \times 15$;

(k) $\frac{1}{4} \times 19 \times 8$;

(l) $\frac{1}{2} \times \frac{1}{3} \times 173 \times 6$;

(m) $(18 \times 11) \div 2$;

(n) $(21 \times 14) \div 3$.

3   Write in a shorter form:

(a) $a + 5 + a$;

(b) $6 + p + 3$;

(c) $b + 5 + b - 3$;

(d) $x + y + x$;

(e) $x + 2y - x$;

(f) $2 \times x \times 5$;

(g) $7 \times p \times 3$;

(h) $3q + 8 - q$;

(i) $n + n + 1 + n + 2$;

(j) $n + 2 + n + n - 2$;

(k) $8a + 3 - 3a$;

(l) $\frac{1}{3} \times a \times 6$;

(m) $\frac{1}{2}d \times 4$;

(n) $4b + 1 - b$;

(o) $51 + 2m + 19 + m$;

(p) $\frac{1}{2}h + \frac{1}{2}h - h$;

(q) $3g + 7 + 2g - 5$;

(r) $6 + 3p + 2p - 5$.

4   Which of the following are correct?

(a) $12 - 7 + 6 = 12 + 6 - 7$;

(b) $(12 \div 6) + 30 = (12 + 30) \div 6$;

(c) $(12 \times 5) \div 6 = (12 \div 6) \times 5$;

(d) $(35 \div 5) \div 7 = (35 \div 7) \div 5$;

(e) $(11 - 7) \times 3 = (11 \times 3) - 7$;

(f) $(12 \div 4) + 2 = (12 + 2) \div 4$;

(g) $15 - 3 - 8 = 15 - 8 - 3$;

(h) $5 \times 9 \times 2 = 5 \times 2 \times 9$;

(i) $(6 + 4) \times 5 = (6 \times 5) + 4$;

(j) $(8 \div 2) \times 6 = (8 \times 6) \div 2$.

Summary

1. An operation $*$ is associative if

$$(a * b) * c \text{ is the same as } a * (b * c)$$

no matter what values we choose for a, b and c.

On the set of numbers the operations of addition and multiplication are associative; for example,

$$(7 + 12) + 3 \quad \text{is the same as} \quad 7 + (12 + 3)$$

and $\qquad (6 \times 7) \times 9 \quad$ is the same as $\quad 6 \times (7 \times 9).$

There is no confusion if we write

$$7 + 12 + 3 \quad \text{and} \quad 6 \times 7 \times 9.$$

2. Brackets are used to indicate which part of an expression must be worked out first.

When an expression contains only $+$ and $-$ and has no brackets, the operations should be performed in the order in which they are written. For example, $\qquad 19 - 5 + 8 \quad$ means $\quad (19 - 5) + 8.$

3. We write:

(i) $(3 \times a) + 4$ as $3a + 4$ and $3 \times (a + 4)$ as $3(a + 4)$;

(ii) $(7 \times a) - 6$ as $7a - 6$ and $7 \times (a - 6)$ as $7(a - 6)$;

(iii) $(a \div 2) + b$ as $\dfrac{a}{2} + b$ and $a \div (2 + b)$ as $\dfrac{a}{2 + b}$;

(iv) $(3 \div a) + 7$ as $\dfrac{3}{a} + 7$ and $3 \div (a + 7)$ as $\dfrac{3}{a + 7}$.

4. When numbers are combined by only $+$ and $-$, we can change the order of the numbers and the operations associated with them. For example, $\qquad 19 - 5 + 8 \quad$ is the same as $\quad 19 + 8 - 5.$

Similarly when numbers are combined by only $\times$ and $\div$, we can change the order of the numbers and the operations associated with them. For example, $\qquad (10 \times 8) \div 2 \quad$ is the same as $\quad (10 \div 2) \times 8.$

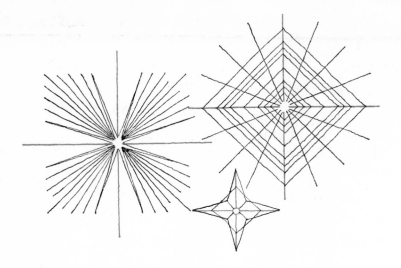

6. Looking at graphs

1. LINEAR RELATIONS

1.1 Graphs of simple linear relations

Investigation 1

On a sheet of graph paper draw two axes so that the origin is roughly in the middle of the paper (see Figure 1 opposite).

(*a*) Find and plot three points which satisfy the relation $y = x$; for example, (1, 1), (3, 3), ($^-3$, $^-3$). Draw the line with equation $y = x$.

(*b*) On the same diagram, draw the lines $y = x+1$, $y = x+2$, $y = x+3$, $y = x+4$, and label these lines with their equations.

(*c*) What do you notice about these lines?

(*d*) Still on the same diagram, draw the lines $y = x-1$, $y = x-2$, $y = x-3$, $y = x-4$.
What do you notice about these lines?

(*e*) You should now be able to draw the following lines straight away:

    (i) $y = x+5$;   (ii) $y = x+6$;

    (iii) $y = x-5$;   (iv) $y = x-7$.

(Do not forget to label all lines you draw with their equations.)

All the lines you have drawn are of the form $y = x+c$.
What does the value of c tell you about the graph?

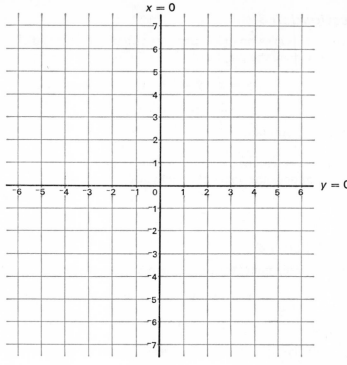

Fig. 1

Investigation 2

Draw two axes on graph paper as you did for Investigation 1.

(a) Find three points satisfying $y = {}^-x$; for example, $(2, {}^-2)$, $(4, {}^-4)$, $({}^-3, 3)$. Draw the line $y = {}^-x$.

(b) Do the same for $y = {}^-x+1$, $y = {}^-x+2$, $y = {}^-x+3$, $y = {}^-x+4$. What do you notice about the lines?

(c) Draw the lines $y = {}^-x-1$, $y = {}^-x-2$, $y = {}^-x-3$, $y = {}^-x-4$. What do you notice about these lines?

(d) Describe in words where you would draw:

  (i) $y = {}^-x+5$;   (ii) $y = {}^-x+8$;

  (iii) $y = {}^-x-6$;   (iv) $y = {}^-x-7$.

How are the lines you have just drawn related to one another?

All these lines are of the form $y = {}^-x+c$.
In what way are they different from the lines you drew in Investigation 1?
What does the value of c tell you?

77

Investigation 3

Draw two axes on graph paper as you did for Investigations 1 and 2.
Now draw the graphs of

$$y = x, \quad y = 2x, \quad y = 3x, \quad y = 4x,$$

$$y = \tfrac{1}{2}x, \quad y = \tfrac{1}{3}x, \quad y = \tfrac{1}{4}x.$$

What do you notice?

These equations are of the form $y = mx$.
What does the value of m tell you?

Investigation 4

On your diagram for Investigation 3, draw the graphs of

$$y = {}^-x, \quad y = {}^-2x, \quad y = {}^-3x, \quad y = {}^-4x,$$

$$y = {}^-\tfrac{1}{2}x, \quad y = {}^-\tfrac{1}{3}x, \quad y = {}^-\tfrac{1}{4}x.$$

What is the connection between the lines $y = 2x$ and $y = {}^-2x$?

What is the connection between the lines $y = 3x$ and $y = {}^-3x$?

What is the connection between the lines $y = \tfrac{1}{4}x$ and $y = {}^-\tfrac{1}{4}x$?

Could you have used the graph of $y = 3x$ to draw the graph of $y = {}^-3x$?

1.2 Graphs of other linear relations

So far you have drawn only the graphs of simple relations: those like
$y = x+3$ or $y = 2x$.

Now let us consider how you would draw the graph of a relation like
$y = 2x+3$. You first need to find some ordered pairs (x, y) which satisfy
the relation.

If $x = 1$, what is y?　　$y = (2 \times 1) + 3 = 5$ giving the point $(1, 5)$.

If $x = 2$, what is y?　　$y = (2 \times 2) + 3 = 4 + 3 = 7$ giving the point
$(2, 7)$.

If $x = {}^-3$, what is y?　$y = (2 \times {}^-3) + 3 = {}^-6 + 3 = {}^-3$ giving the point
$({}^-3, {}^-3)$.

Figure 2 shows the graph of the relation $y = 2x + 3$.

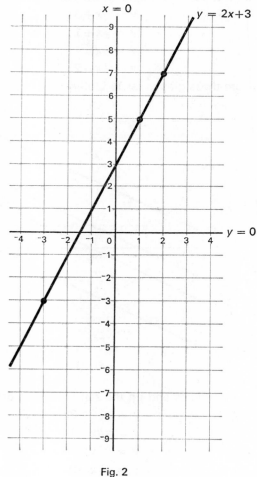

Fig. 2

(*a*) Check first by calculation and then by looking at the graph that the following points satisfy the relation:

$$(0, 3), \quad (3, 9), \quad (^-1, 1), \quad (^-2, ^-1).$$

(*b*) Copy Figure 2 onto a sheet of graph paper and on the same sheet, draw the graphs of $y = 2x + 5$, $y = 2x - 1$, $y = 2x - 2$.

What do you notice? Is this what you would have expected?

Exercise A

1   Figure 3 shows the graphs of the relations:
$$y = \tfrac{1}{2}x + 3;$$
$$y = \tfrac{1}{2}x + 1;$$
$$y = \tfrac{1}{2}x;$$
$$y = \tfrac{1}{2}x - 2.$$

How are these graphs related to each other?

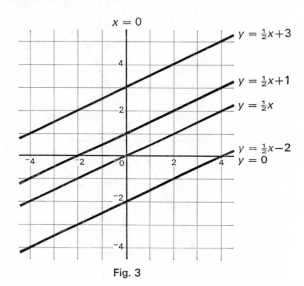

Fig. 3

Copy these lines and on the same diagram draw the graphs of the relations:
$$y = -\tfrac{1}{2}x + 3;$$
$$y = -\tfrac{1}{2}x + 1;$$
$$y = -\tfrac{1}{2}x;$$
$$y = -\tfrac{1}{2}x - 2.$$

How are these graphs related (a) to each other; (b) to the set of graphs in Figure 3?

2   Figure 4 (opposite) shows the graph of the relation $y = 2x - 3$. The dotted lines show how the graph can be used to solve the equation
$$2x - 3 = 5,$$
giving $\qquad\qquad\qquad x = 4.$

Use the graph to solve:

(a) $2x - 3 = 3$;   (b) $2x - 3 = 7$;   (c) $2x - 3 = 0$;
(d) $2x - 3 = {}^{-}7$;   (e) $2x - 3 = {}^{-}2$;   (f) $2x - 3 = {}^{-}6$.

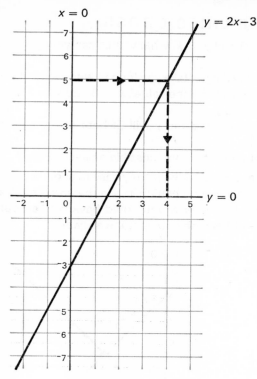

Fig. 4

3 Draw the graph of $y = 3x+2$, choosing values of x between $^-3$ and 2 ($^-3 \leqslant x \leqslant 2$). (You will need to mark your $y = 0$ axis from $^-3$ to 2 and your $x = 0$ axis from $^-7$ to 8.)

Use your graph to solve the equations:

(*a*) $3x+2 = ^-1$;   (*b*) $3x+2 = 5$;   (*c*) $3x+2 = ^-7$;

(*d*) $3x+2 = 8$;   (*e*) $3x+2 = 6\frac{1}{2}$;   (*f*) $3x+2 = \frac{1}{2}$.

4 Mark out a sheet of graph paper for values of x and y between 0 and 12

Draw the following graphs:

(*a*) $x+y = 4$;   (*b*) $x+y = 6$;

(*c*) $x+y = 7$;   (*d*) $x+y = 10$.

You should now see where to draw the next graphs without doing any working:

(*e*) $x+y = 9$;   (*f*) $x+y = 5$;

(*g*) $x+y = 12$;   (*h*) $x+y = 1$.

2. WHERE LINES CROSS

If $x+y = 6$ and $y = x$, what values can you give to x and y that fit both equations?

It probably did not take you long to work out that x and y must both be 3.

We could say that the values $x = 3$ and $y = 3$ fit both of the equations $x+y = 6$ and $y = x$.

What values of x and y will fit both of the equations $x+y = 10$ and $y = x$?

Is there more than one possible answer to this?

These two answers were very easy to spot, but you might have pairs of equations where you could not see the answers so easily.

Figure 5 shows how you could have worked out the last question if you had not been able to spot the answer.

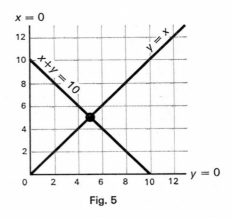

Fig. 5

The lines for $x+y = 10$ and $y = x$ cross at the point (5, 5). This means that the point (5, 5) lies on both lines. Does any other point lie on both lines?

(5, 5) is just a quick way of writing 'the point where the value of x is 5 and the value of y is 5', so this shows that the values $x = 5$ and $y = 5$ fit both of the equations $x+y = 10$ and $y = x$.

Exercise B

For Questions 1 and 2, mark your axes like those in Figure 5.

1 Draw the lines $x+y = 6$ and $y = 2x$ on the same diagram. Give the values of x and y which fit both these equations.

2 Draw graphs to find which values of x and y fit both of the equations $x+y = 8$ and $y = 3x$.

3   Mark axes for $0 \leqslant x \leqslant 6$ and $0 \leqslant y \leqslant 12$.
Draw the lines $y = x+3$ and $y = 2x-1$. What values of x and y fit both these equations?

4   Mark your axes as for Question 3. Draw graphs to find which values of x and y fit both of the equations $y = 2x+3$ and $y = 4x$.

5   Copy the line $y = 2x-3$ from Figure 4. On the same diagram draw the line $y = 5$. What are the coordinates of the point where the lines meet?
Do these values of x and y fit both of the equations $y = 2x-3$ and $y = 5$?

3. EQUATIONS WHICH DO NOT GIVE STRAIGHT LINES (NON-LINEAR RELATIONS)

Not all equations will give you a straight line graph.
Copy and complete this table:

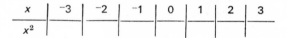

x	-3	-2	-1	0	1	2	3
x^2							

You can probably do the last four easily enough, but be careful with the first three.
How will this table help you to draw the graph of $y = x^2$?
Some of the points on this graph will be (0, 0), (1, 1), (2, 4), etc.
Mark axes for $-3 \leqslant x \leqslant 3$ and $0 \leqslant y \leqslant 9$.
Draw the graph of $y = x^2$. You should get a curve—join the points to give a good smooth curve and not a jerky series of straight lines.

Exercise C

1   On the diagram with the curve $y = x^2$, draw the line $y = 4$.
What happens? Can you explain this?

2   In Question 1 you should have found that two sets of values of x and y fitted the equations $y = x^2$ and $y = 4$.
On the same diagram draw the line $y = x+2$.
What two sets of values of x and y fit both of the equations $y = x^2$ and $y = x+2$?

3   Draw the graph of $y = x^2+2$ for $-3 \leqslant x \leqslant 3$. (Work out a table of values first and so see what values of y you will need.)

Exercise D (Miscellaneous)

1   Draw the line $y = 4 + {}^-3x$ for ${}^-2 \leqslant x \leqslant 3$ and ${}^-5 \leqslant y \leqslant 10$.
Solve the equations:

(a) $4 + {}^-3x = 1$;   (b) $4 + {}^-3x = {}^-2$;   (c) $4 + {}^-3x = 7$.

2   *Answer this question without drawing any graphs.* (If you have difficulty look back at the Investigations you did at the beginning of the chapter.)

(a) Where will the line $y = 3x - 1$ cross the $x = 0$ axis?
(b) Put these lines in order of steepness:

$y = 3x + 2$, $y = 2x - 4$, $y = \frac{1}{2}x - 10$, $y = 4x + 5$.

(c) What can you say about the lines $y = 2x - 3$ and $y = {}^-2x + 6$?
(d) Write down the equations of three lines which will be parallel to the line $y = 4x + 1$.

3   *Another investigation*
Draw the lines $y = 2x + 1$ and $y = {}^-\frac{1}{2}x + 1$ on the same diagram. (Use axes as in Figure 1.) Measure the angle between the two lines.
    On a new diagram draw the lines $y = 3x + 2$ and $y = {}^-\frac{1}{3}x + 2$ and measure the angle between them.
    Do the same for the following pairs of lines:

(a) $y = \frac{1}{2}x + 3$ and $y = {}^-2x - 1$;
(b) $y = \frac{1}{2}x + 2$ and $y = 3x - 1$;
(c) $y = \frac{1}{3}x - 4$ and $y = 3x + 1$;
(d) $y = 4x + 3$ and $y = {}^-\frac{1}{4}x + 2$.

Look at the pairs of equations which gave lines at right-angles to each other.

Can you see a connection between the two equations in each of these cases?

Revision exercises

Quick quiz, no. 1

1 (a) $\frac{3}{4} \times 8$;   (b) $\frac{3}{4} \div 8$.

2 A line segment joins (0, 0) to (4, 2). What is its equation?

3 If $a = 3$ and $b = 4$, find the value of
   (a) $a(a+b)$;   (b) $a^2 - ab - b^2$.

4 What is the image of (⁻1, 2) in the mirror line $y = x$?

5 Give the inverse under addition of
   (a) ⁻5;   (b) ⁺3;   (c) 0.

6 A line segment of length $3\frac{1}{2}$ cm is enlarged by a scale factor of 3. What is its new length?

Quick quiz, no. 2

1 Insert the correct sign in the following:
   (a) $2 \quad \frac{1}{5} = 10$;   (b) $\frac{4}{5} \quad \frac{1}{10} = \frac{9}{10}$;   (c) $\frac{2}{7} \quad \frac{3}{4} = \frac{6}{28}$.

2 A translation has vector $\begin{pmatrix} -1 \\ 2 \end{pmatrix}$. Onto what points would the translation map the following points?
   (a) (1, ⁻2);   (b) (⁻1, ⁻4).

3 Which of the following lines pass through the origin?
   $$y = x+2, \quad y = x, \quad y = 2x, \quad y = x-2, \quad y = {}^{-}2x.$$

4 Write in shorter form:
   (a) $6p - p + 2q - 6q$;   (b) $\frac{1}{2} \times 2p \times 3$.

5 How many 5 cm squares will fit inside a 1 m square?

6 How many planes of symmetry has a cuboid?

Computation 1

1 $2+4+6+8+92+94+96+98$.

2 $3 \cdot 33 \times 27 \cdot 4$.

3 Find the mean of 99, 98, 105, 103, 94, 101.

4 $667{\cdot}94 \div 1{\cdot}3$.

5 $(4 \times 2) + (5 \times 2) + (6 \times 2) + (7 \times 2) + (8 \times 2)$.

6 $25 \times 33 \times 4 \times 30$.

Exercise A

1 A girl saves one-third of her pocket money and spends three-quarters of what she has left on sweets. What fraction of her total pocket money does she spend on sweets?

2 An octagon has $x = 0$, $y = 0$ and $y = x$ as lines of symmetry. Draw these lines for values of x and y between $^-4$ and 4.

  (2, 3) is a vertex. Find the other vertices and write down their coordinates. Has the polygon any other lines of symmetry? If so, give the equations of these lines.

3

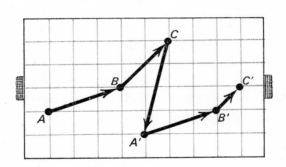

Fig. 1

Figure 1 shows a diagram of a soccer pitch and the path taken by a ball as it is passed from Alan to Bob, Bob to Chris, Chris back to Alan, Alan to Bob again and finally from Bob to Chris, who scores a goal. If each square on the grid represents 10 m, then the vector describing the first pass can be written as $\begin{pmatrix} 30 \\ 10 \end{pmatrix}$.

  Write down the other passes as vectors. Add them together. Do you get the result you would have expected?

  Write down also the three vectors which describe the change of position of each of the three boys.

4 If $a * b$ means $2a + b$, work out

(a) $4 * 3$;   (b) $5 * {}^-5$;   (c) $3(2 * 1)$;   (d) $2 * (1 * 3)$.

5

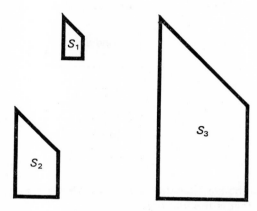

Fig. 2

Copy Figure 2.

(a) Find the centre of enlargement which maps S_1 onto S_2.

(b) Find the centre of enlargement which maps S_2 onto S_3.

(c) Find the centre of enlargement which maps S_1 onto S_3.

What do you notice about the 3 centres of enlargement?

Exercise B

1 A rectangle measures $2\frac{1}{2}$ cm by $3\frac{1}{4}$ cm. What is its total perimeter and its area? If it is divided into a square of side $2\frac{1}{2}$ cm and another rectangle, what are the dimensions of this smaller rectangle and what is its area?

2 If

$$\mathbf{a} = \begin{pmatrix} 2 \\ 3 \\ 1 \end{pmatrix}, \quad \mathbf{b} = \begin{pmatrix} 3 \\ 4 \\ 5 \end{pmatrix}, \quad \mathbf{c} = \begin{pmatrix} 0 \\ 1 \\ 2 \end{pmatrix},$$

find

(a) $\mathbf{a} + \mathbf{b}$;   (b) $2\mathbf{c}$;   (c) $\mathbf{b} - \mathbf{a}$;

(d) $2(\mathbf{b} + \mathbf{c})$;   (e) $\frac{1}{2}(\mathbf{b} + \mathbf{c})$;   (f) $3\mathbf{b} + \mathbf{c}$.

3   The operation $*$ is defined on the set $\{2, 4, 6, 8\}$ by the relation

$a * b =$ the units digit in the product $a \times b$.

(For example, $4 * 8 = 2$, because 2 is the units digits of 32.)
Complete the following combination table.

	Second element			
$*$	2	4	6	8
2				
4				
6				
8				

First element

(a) Is the set closed under the operation $*$?
(b) What is the identity?
(c) What is the inverse of

    (i) 2,   (ii) 4,   (iii) 6,   (iv) 8?

4   The lines $y = 2$ and $x = 3$ are two lines of symmetry of a polygon. Four of its vertices have coordinates $(3, 8)$, $(2, 6)$, $(^-1, 3)$, $(^-3, 2)$.
    Find the coordinates of its other vertices, and draw the complete polygon. Mark clearly any other lines of symmetry of the polygon (if any) and write down their equations. (Take 1 cm to 1 unit along both axes for $^-4 \leqslant x \leqslant 10$ and $^-5 \leqslant y \leqslant 9$.)
    What is the centre of rotational symmetry and order of rotational symmetry of the polygon?

5   Suppose 'S' means 'take the smaller number from the larger number'. Then $7 \, S \, 4 = 3$ and $4 \, S \, 7 = 3$. Is the operation S commutative?
    Work out (a) $(8 \, S \, 13) \, S \, 2$; (b) $8 \, S \, (13 \, S \, 2)$.
    Is the operation associative? Try other triples of numbers.

Exercise C

1   If $a = {}^-3$, find the value of:

(a) $2a$;

(b) ^-6a;

(c) $4a + 5$;

(d) a^2;

(e) $^-\frac{1}{2}a$;

(f) $^-2a^2$;

(g) a^3;

(h) $5(a+1)$;

(i) $\frac{1}{5}(3a - 1)$.

2 In a class of 28 pupils, 21 clean their teeth every morning. What fraction of the whole class is this? If there are 15 girls and $\frac{3}{5}$ of them clean their teeth every morning, what fraction of the boys do the same?

3

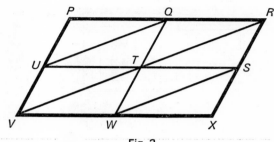

Fig. 3

(*a*) What centre of enlargement maps triangle *PQU* onto triangle *PRV*? What is the scale factor of this enlargement?
(*b*) Copy Figure 3 and *construct* the centre of enlargement that maps *PQU* onto *XVR*. What is the scale factor of this enlargement?

4 Describe how you could map triangle *PQU* onto *each* of the small triangles in Figure 3 by a single change of position.

5 Copy and complete the following table for the set $\{-2, -1, 0, 1, 2\}$ under subtraction.

		Second number				
	$-$	-2	-1	0	1	2
	-2	0	-1	-2	-3	
First number	-1		0			
	0		1			
	1		2			
	2					

Is the set $\{-2, -1, 0, 1, 2\}$ closed under subtraction?
Does the set contain an identity for subtraction?
Does each member of the set have an inverse?
Give reasons for your answers.

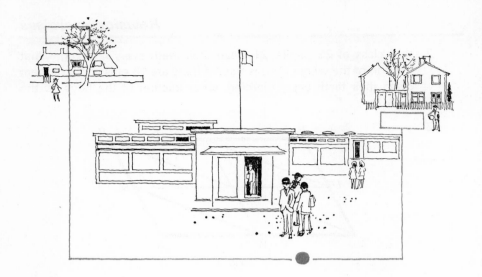

7. Ratio

1. WHAT IS A RATIO?

Consider the statement:

'Mary lives twice as far from school as John'.

(*a*) Do you know who lives nearer to the school?

(*b*) Do you know the distance in kilometres from John's home to school?

(*c*) Do you know the distance in kilometres from Mary's home to school?

(*d*) Copy and complete the following table which shows some possible distances that Mary and John could live from school:

Distance from Mary's home to school in kilometres	10			4			$1\frac{1}{2}$		$\frac{1}{2}$
Distance from John's home to school in kilometres	5	4	3	2	$1\frac{1}{2}$	1	$\frac{3}{4}$	$\frac{1}{2}$	$\frac{1}{4}$

When we say that Mary's distance is twice John's distance, we are comparing the two distances. We do not know the actual distance from John's home to school, but if we call it 1 unit then Mary's distance is 2 of those units.

We can compare the distances by using a fraction and write

$$\frac{\text{Mary's distance}}{\text{John's distance}} = \frac{2}{1}, \quad \text{or simply 2.}$$

We can also compare the distances by using a *ratio* and say that the ratio of Mary's distance to John's distance is *'two to one'* or 2 to 1.

We could call John's distance 5 units of some other kind. Then Mary's distance would be 10 of these units and so we could say that

$$\frac{\text{Mary's distance}}{\text{John's distance}} = \frac{10}{5}$$

and the ratio of Mary's distance to John's distance is 10 to 5.

(*e*) Would it be correct to say that $\dfrac{\text{Mary's distance}}{\text{John's distance}} = \dfrac{4}{2}$?

(*f*) Would it be correct to say that Mary's distance to John's distance is 4 to 2?

(*g*) Write down the ratio of Mary's distance to John's distance in six other ways.

(*h*) What can you say about the following fractions?

$$\frac{10}{5}, \frac{8}{4}, \frac{6}{3}, \frac{4}{2}, \frac{3}{1\frac{1}{2}}, \frac{2}{1}, \frac{1\frac{1}{2}}{\frac{3}{4}}, \frac{1}{\frac{1}{2}} \quad \text{and} \quad \frac{\frac{1}{2}}{\frac{1}{4}}.$$

Which is the simplest of these fractions?

(*i*) What can you say about the following ratios?

10 to 5, 8 to 4, 6 to 3, 4 to 2, 3 to $1\frac{1}{2}$, 2 to 1, $1\frac{1}{2}$ to $\frac{3}{4}$, 1 to $\frac{1}{2}$ and $\frac{1}{2}$ to $\frac{1}{4}$.

Which do you think is the simplest of these ratios?

(*j*) What would it mean if we said that the ratio of Mary's distance to John's distance is 1 to 2? Who would live further from the school?

Exercise A

1 Consider the statement: 'Peter's pencil is three times as long as Anne's'.

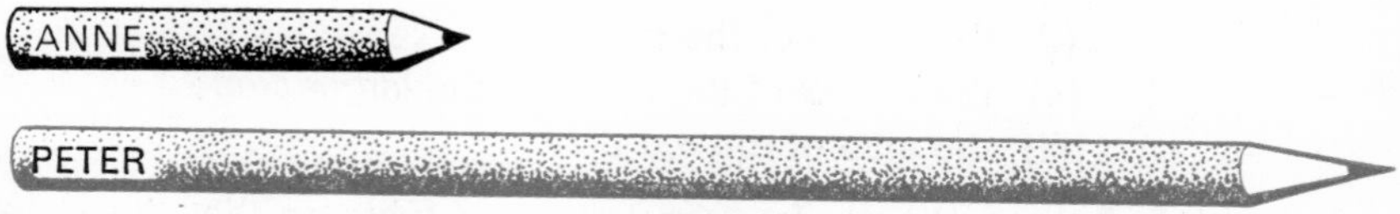

Fig. 1

(*a*) One possible pair of pencils is shown in Figure 1. Copy and complete the following table which shows some other possible pencil lengths:

Length of Peter's pencil in cm					
Length of Anne's pencil in cm	6	7	8	9	10

(*b*) Write the fraction $\dfrac{\text{Peter's pencil length}}{\text{Anne's pencil length}}$ in five different ways.

(*c*) Write the ratio of Peter's pencil length to Anne's pencil length in five different ways.

(*d*) Write both the fraction and the ratio as simply as you can.

2

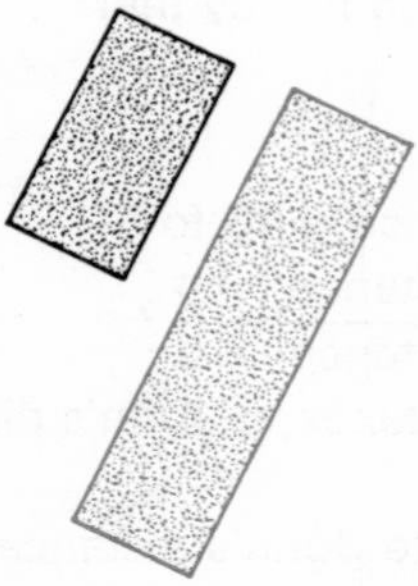

Fig. 2 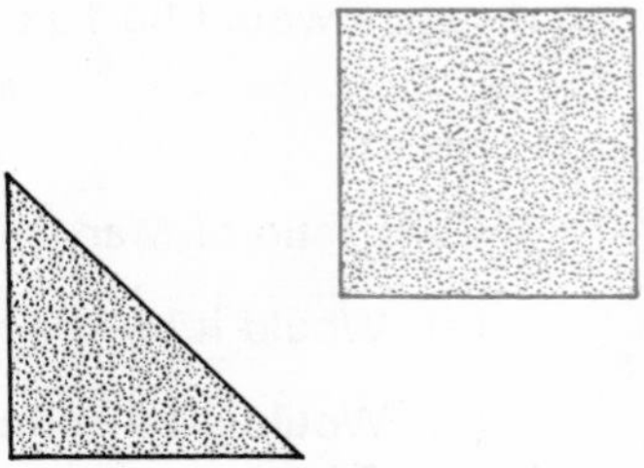   Fig. 3

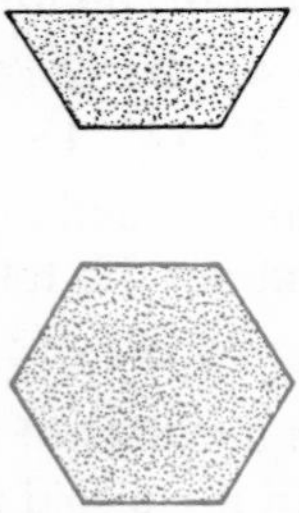

Fig. 4

Consider the statement: 'the black tile is half the area of the red tile'.

(*a*) Some possible pairs of tiles are shown in Figures 2, 3 and 4. Does the statement tell you:

    (i) the shape of the black tile;

    (ii) the colour of the tile with the larger area;

    (iii) the area of the red tile?

(*b*) Copy and complete the following table so that the statement is true:

Area of black tile in cm²						
Area of red tile in cm²	10	16	25	32	100	400

(*c*) Write the fraction $\dfrac{\text{area of black tile}}{\text{area of red tile}}$ in six different ways.

(*d*) Write the ratio of the area of the black tile to the area of the red tile in six different ways.

(*e*) Write both the fraction and the ratio as simply as you can.

(*f*) What is the value of the fraction $\dfrac{\text{area of red tile}}{\text{area of black tile}}$?

(*g*) What is the ratio of the area of the red tile to the area of the black tile?

3 Consider the statement: 'the apple tree is one-quarter the height of the oak tree.'

(*a*) Copy and complete the following table which shows some possible heights of the trees:

Height of apple tree in metres						
Height of oak tree in metres	10	12	14	16	18	20

(*b*) What is the ratio of the height of the apple tree to the height of the oak tree? Write your answer as simply as you can.

(*c*) What is the ratio of the height of the oak tree to the height of the apple tree?

2. SIMPLEST FORMS

(*a*)

Fig. 5

Copy and fill in the missing numbers:

$$\frac{8}{12} = \frac{4}{-} = \frac{}{3}.$$

(*b*)

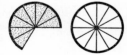

Fig. 6

Copy and fill in the missing numbers:

8 to 12 = 4 to   =   to 3.

93

A fraction is in its simplest form when the two numbers forming the fraction (the top and bottom numbers) are whole numbers which have no common factor.

(*c*) Copy and complete the following example.

Example 1

Write as simply as you can:

$$\text{(i) } \frac{4}{8}; \quad \text{(ii) } \frac{25}{10}; \quad \text{(iii) } \frac{\frac{1}{3}}{2}.$$

(i) Dividing 4 and 8 by 4, $\frac{4}{8} = \underline{\quad}.$

(ii) Dividing 25 and 10 by 5, $\frac{25}{10} = \underline{\quad}.$

(iii) Multiplying $\frac{1}{3}$ and 2 by 3, $\frac{\frac{1}{3}}{2} = \underline{\quad}.$

A ratio is also in its simplest form when the two numbers forming the ratio are whole numbers which have no common factor.

(*d*) Copy and complete Example 2.

Example 2

Write as simply as you can:

(i) 4 to 8;   (ii) 25 to 10;   (iii) $\frac{1}{3}$ to 2.

(i) Dividing 4 and 8 by 4,   4 to 8 =   .

(ii) Dividing 25 and 10 by 5,   25 to 10 =   .

(iii) Multiplying $\frac{1}{3}$ and 2 by 3, $\frac{1}{3}$ to 2 =   .

Exercise B

1   Copy and fill in the missing numbers:

(*a*) $\dfrac{60}{80} = \dfrac{}{20} = \dfrac{3}{\_};$

(*b*) 60 to 80 =   to 20 = 3 to   ;

(*c*) $\dfrac{90}{150} = \dfrac{9}{\_} = \dfrac{}{5};$

(*d*) 90 to 150 = 9 to   =   to 5.

2 Write the following fractions in their simplest form:

(a) $\frac{6}{10}$; (b) $\frac{16}{32}$; (c) $\frac{9}{27}$; (d) $\frac{14}{21}$;

(e) $\frac{18}{90}$; (f) $\frac{24}{30}$; (g) $\frac{2000}{5000}$; (h) $\frac{90}{360}$.

3 Write the following ratios in their simplest form:

(a) 2 to 10; (b) 80 to 20; (c) $\frac{1}{3}$ to 1;

(d) 2 to $2\frac{1}{2}$; (e) 12 to 120; (f) £3 to £15;

(g) 100 kg to 50 kg; (h) $\frac{1}{4}$ to $\frac{3}{4}$; (i) £0·50 to £5;

(j) 60 m to 15 m; (k) $1\frac{1}{2}$ to 1; (l) $\frac{4}{3}$ to 3;

(m) 2 shovels full of cement to 6 shovels full of gravel;
(n) 8 cupfuls of water to 12 cupfuls of flour.

4 Say which of the following statements are true and which are false. If any are false, correct them.

(a) The ratio of 4 to 2 is equivalent to 2 to 1.
(b) The ratio of $\frac{1}{4}$ to 1 is equivalent to 1 to 3.
(c) The ratio of 20 to 10 is equivalent to 10 to 5. This is the same as 5 to 1.
(d) If the ratio of my pocket money to my brother's is 3 to 1, then he gets three times as much money as I do.
(e) If the ratio of my pocket money to my brother's is 3 to 1, then the ratio of my brother's pocket money to mine is 1 to 3.
(f) If the ratio of Edgar's age to Fiona's age is 5 to 3, then Fiona's age is $\frac{3}{5}$ of Edgar's age.
(g) If the ratio of Edgar's age to Fiona's age is 5 to 3, then the ratio of Fiona's age to Edgar's age is also 5 to 3.

5 Mary lives twice as far from school as John.

(a) If John and Mary walk to school at the same speed, what can you say about the times they take?
(b) If John and Mary walk to school in the same time, what can you say about their speeds?

6 The ratio of my weight to my brother's weight is 2 to 1. If I weigh 80 kg, how much does my brother weigh?

7 In a certain class the ratio of boys to girls is 1 to 2. If there are 10 boys, how many girls are there?

8 In another class there are 36 boys and only 12 girls. Write the ratio of boys to girls in its simplest form. What is the ratio of girls to boys?

9

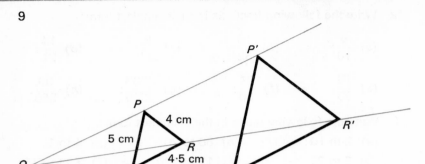

Fig. 7

In Figure 7, triangle *PQR* is mapped onto triangle *P'Q'R'* by an enlargement centre *O* and scale factor 2.

(*a*) State the lengths of (i) *P'Q'*; (ii) *Q'R'*; (iii) *R'P'*.

(*b*) Write down the ratios of (*i*) *P'Q'* to *PQ*; (ii) *QR* to *Q'R'*.

10

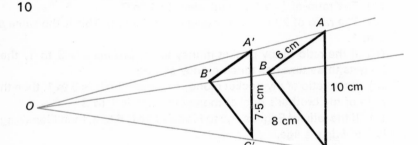

Fig. 8

In Figure 8, the triangle *ABC* is mapped onto triangle *A'B'C'* by an enlargement centre *O*.

(*a*) State the ratio of (i) *A'C'* to *AC*; (ii) *B'C'* to *BC*; (iii) *A'B'* to *AB*.

(*b*) Find the lengths of *B'C'* and *A'B'*.

11 A cake is divided so that one person gets three times as much as the other. Write down the ratio of the smaller share to the larger one. If the smaller share is 30 g, what is the larger one?

12 There are 25 teachers in a school of 500 pupils. Find the teacher to pupil ratio in its simplest form. What is the ratio of teachers to pupils in your school?

13 In a school of 420 pupils, 20 are prefects. What is the ratio of prefects to non-prefects?

14 In a certain county it was decided that schools with 600 children should have 40 teachers and that the ratio of children to teachers should be the same for every school in the county.

(*a*) What is this ratio in its simplest form?

(*b*) Would the headmaster of a school with 315 children and 20 teachers have to employ more staff? If so, how many?

(*c*) Working with this ratio of 600 children to 40 teachers, would it be necessary for your headteacher to employ more staff or dismiss some? Find how many.

15

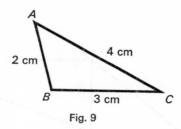

Fig. 9

The triangle *ABC* in Figure 9 is enlarged. Write down the lengths of the sides of the new triangle if

(*a*) the shortest side becomes 10 cm long;

(*b*) the longest side becomes 6 cm long.

16

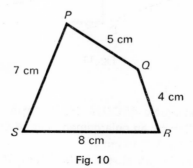

Fig. 10

The quadrilateral *PQRS* in Figure 10 is enlarged. Write down the lengths of the sides of the new quadrilateral if

(*a*) the shortest side becomes 10 cm long;

(*b*) the longest side becomes 2 cm long.

3. USING THE SAME UNITS

(*a*) David finished his Mathematics homework in 25 minutes, but his Geography took 1¼ hours.

Why would it be wrong to say that the ratio of time spent on Mathematics to the time spent on Geography is 25 to 1¼?

When we use a ratio to compare two quantities we must write both quantities in the same units.

How many minutes did David spend on Geography?
What is the ratio of time spent on Mathematics to time spent on Geography?

(*b*)

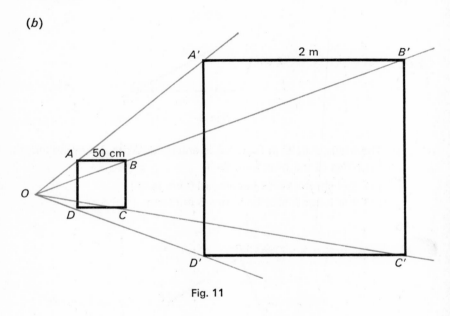

Fig. 11

In Figure 11, the square *ABCD* of side 50 cm is mapped onto the square *A'B'C'D'* of side 2 m by an enlargement, centre *O*.

State the length of *A'B'* in cm.

What is the ratio : length of *A'B'* to length of *AB*? Write this ratio in its simplest form.

Write down the ratios:

(i) $B'C'$ to BC;

(ii) $C'D'$ to CD;

(iii) $D'A'$ to DA.

What is the scale factor of the enlargement?

Could $A'B'C'D'$ be mapped onto $ABCD$ by an enlargement? What scale factor would be needed?

Write down the ratios:

(i) BC to $B'C'$;

(ii) AB to $A'B'$;

(iii) BD to $B'D'$.

Exercise C

1   Say which of the following statements are true and which are false. If any are false, correct them.

(*a*) The ratio of 10 kg to 2 kg is 10 to 2. This can be written more simply as 5 to 1.

(*b*) The ratio of an hour to a quarter of an hour is 4 to 1.

(*c*) The ratio of an hour to 30 minutes is 1 to 30.

(*d*) The ratio of 4 days to 1 week is 4 to 7.

(*e*) The ratio of 1 metre to 1 centimetre is 100 to 1.

(*f*) The ratio of 1 g to 1 kg is 1 to 1.

(*g*) The ratio of 3 minutes to 3 hours is 3 to 3.

(*h*) The ratio of 100 m to 1 km is 1 to 10.

2   Write the following ratios in their simplest form:

(*a*) 1 week to 1 day;   (*b*) 6 days to 3 weeks;

(*c*) 10 m to 1 km;   (*d*) 3 hours to 1 day;

(*e*) 5 kg to 50 kg;   (*f*) 10 minutes to 4 hours;

(*g*) 75p to £1;   (*h*) £5 to 40p.

3   (*a*) John and Henry earn their pocket money by doing odd jobs. One week, Henry earns 90p and John earns £3. What is the ratio of Henry's earnings to John's earnings? What is the ratio of John's earnings to Henry's earnings?

(*b*) Henry works for 50 minutes and John works for 5 hours. What is the ratio of Henry's time to John's time?

4. SHARING

(*a*)

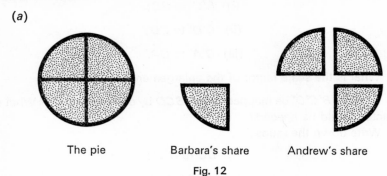

| The pie | Barbara's share | Andrew's share |

Fig. 12

A pie is divided between Andrew and Barbara so that Andrew has three times as much as Barbara.

What is the ratio of Andrew's share to Barbara's share?

Figure 12 shows that the pie is cut into equal slices and that Barbara is given one of these slices. How many are given to Andrew? How many slices are there altogether?

What fraction of the pie is given to Barbara? What fraction is given to Andrew?

(*b*) Another pie is to be divided between Charles and Diana in the ratio 3 to 5.

Into how many equal slices would you cut this pie? How many of these slices would you give to Charles?

What fraction of the pie should be given to Charles? What fraction should Diana have?

(*c*) Three 'pop' groups, the Whackers, the Crackers and the Backers performed at a school concert. The pupils voted for their favourite group and the pie chart representing the result of the votes is shown in Figure 13.

Which was the most popular group?

Copy and complete the following statements:

(i) number of votes for the Whackers to number of votes for the Crackers = 210 to ...;

(ii) number of votes for the Crackers to number of votes for the Backers = ... to 60;

(iii) number of votes for the Whackers to number of votes for the Crackers to number of votes for the Backers is ... to 90 to .... Write this ratio as simply as you can.

What fraction of the votes cast did each group receive?

Six hundred pupils voted. How many votes did each group receive?

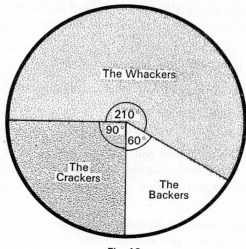

Fig. 13

(*d*) 80p is divided between three sisters, Jane, Kate and Linda in the ratio of their ages. Jane is 5 years old, Kate is 6 and Linda is 9.
Copy and complete the following:

Jane's age to Kate's age to Linda's age is ... to ... to ....

The sum of their ages is ....

Jane gets $\frac{5}{20}$ of 80p = $\frac{5}{20} \times$ 80p = ... p.

Kate gets ... of 80p = ... p = ... p.

Linda gets .... = ... = ...

Check that your three answers add to 80p.

Exercise D

In questions which ask you to divide a quantity into a number of parts, check that the parts add to give the whole quantity.

1

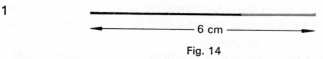

Fig. 14

A straight line segment 6 cm long is divided into two parts in the ratio 2 to 1. What fraction of the line segment is the longer part? How long is the longer part?

2 60 foreign stamps are to be divided between Bill and his younger sister. Bill, who is a keen collector, is to get twice as many as his sister. How many does his sister get?

3 800 kilogrammes of coal are divided between two families in the ratio 2 to 3. How much coal does each family receive?

4 There is four times as much nitrogen as oxygen in air. How much oxygen is there in 25 litres of air?

5 Divide £60 between Alan, Hilary and Isobel in the ratio 5 to 3 to 2.

6 Four shareholders hold 300, 100, 500 and 600 shares respectively in a company. Divide £7500 between them in the ratio of their holdings.

7 Magnesium combines with oxygen in the ratio 3 parts to 2 parts by weight. How much magnesium would be needed to combine with 1·4 kg of oxygen? What would be the weight of the substance formed?

8 Calor gas contains 19 parts butane and 1 part propane by volume. How much calor gas can be made from 1000 litres of propane if there is an unlimited supply of butane?

9 Blue copper sulphate is made from:

> 32 parts of copper,
> 16 parts of sulphur,
> 32 parts of oxygen,
> 45 parts of water.

(a) How much water is there in 5 kg of copper sulphate?

(b) How much copper sulphate could be made with 96 kg of copper?

10 Do you receive more land as the junior partner in a 3 to 2 share out of 0·085 km^2, or as the senior partner in a 4 to 1 share out of 0·045 km^2? How much more would you get?

11 Divide 360° into 4 angles in the ratio 1 to 2 to 3 to 4.

12 In a certain week a boy spent 5p on chocolate, 10p on fares, 15p on stamps and 20p on a visit to the cinema. Write down and simplify the ratio of these sums of money. He wishes to draw a pie chart to illustrate his spending. Use the ratio to help you to find the sector angles and draw the pie chart.

  Draw a pie chart to illustrate how you spent *your* pocket money last week.

13 Find out the number of hours on a certain day that B.B.C. 1

(a) broadcasts to schools,

(b) is used for other broadcasting,

(c) is off the air.

Represent this information on a pie chart.

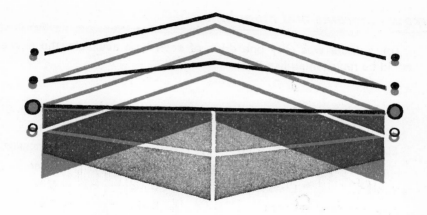

8. Arrow diagrams and mappings

1. ARROW DIAGRAMS

(a) Figure 1 shows a relation between a set of people and the drinks they had on a certain day.

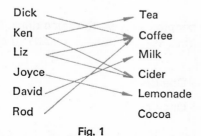

Fig. 1

The relation shows which drinks each person had on that day.

(b) Here is another relation between the same two sets.

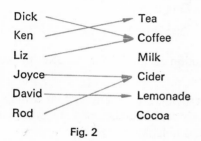

Fig. 2

This relation shows the favourite drink of each person.

(*c*) If there was only one drink of each type available, the relation could be represented like this:

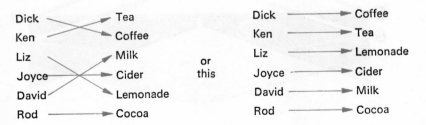

Fig. 3

Look at the arrow patterns and see what differences you notice between the three situations.

(i)   In the first example we have

Many (more than one) persons → One drink

and   One person → Many drinks.

This relation has a MANY to MANY correspondence.

(ii)   In the second example, two people can have the same drink, but no person can have more than one drink. We say there is a MANY to ONE correspondence for this relation.

Many persons → One drink

(Many arrows → One drink)

(iii) The third example gives us the simplest relation of the three. Each person has one drink only, and no person can have the same drink. We say there is a ONE to ONE correspondence for this relation.

One person → One drink

(One arrow → One drink)

(iv) Can you think of a situation suitable for a ONE to MANY correspondence?

Which of these relations are mappings? (Remember that a mapping is a special kind of relation in which each member of the starting set is related to exactly one member of the finishing set.)

Exercise A

1

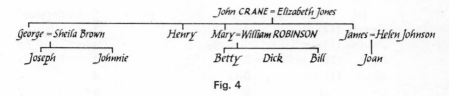

Fig. 4

(*a*)

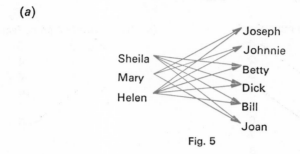

Fig. 5

Figure 5 shows the relation 'is the aunt of'.
What type of correspondence is there between the members of each set?

(*b*) Draw an arrow diagram to show the relation 'is the brother of' for the set of grandchildren of John Crane (see Figure 4). What type of correspondence is there?

(*c*) Draw an arrow diagram to show the relation 'is the sister of' for the set of grandchildren of John Crane.

   What type of correspondence is there this time?

   Does it make any difference to the type of correspondence if you include the children of John Crane in your set?

   Describe a situation which *will* alter the type of correspondence.

2 The following relations refer to the whole family of Figure 4. In each case, describe what type of correspondence there is. (You may find it helpful to draw the arrow diagrams.)

   (*a*) 'is the father of';
   (*b*) 'is the parent of';
   (*c*) 'is the uncle of';
   (*d*) 'is the grandfather of';
   (*e*) 'is the cousin of'.

3   Complete the following arrow diagrams and decide whether they represent many to many, many to one, one to many, or one to one relations.

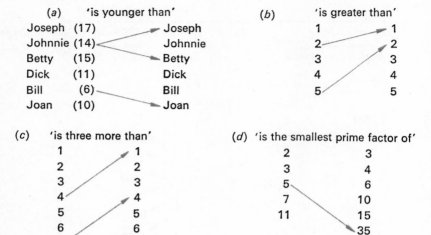

(a)   'is younger than'

Joseph (17)   Joseph
Johnnie (14)   Johnnie
Betty   (15)   Betty
Dick   (11)   Dick
Bill   (6)   Bill
Joan   (10)   Joan

(b)   'is greater than'

1   1
2   2
3   3
4   4
5   5

(c)   'is three more than'

1   1
2   2
3   3
4   4
5   5
6   6
7   7
8   8

(d)   'is the smallest prime factor of'

2   3
3   4
5   6
7   10
11   15
     35

Fig. 6

4   Draw a diagram to represent the relation 'is a factor of' between the sets {2, 3, 4, 5} and {20, 21, 22, 23, 24}.
    What type of relation is it?

5   Draw a diagram between the sets {20, 21, 22, 23, 24} and {1, 2, 3, 4, 5} for the relation 'has this number of prime factors'. (Remember that 1 is not a prime number.)

2. MAPPING DIAGRAMS

Here are some relations involving numbers:

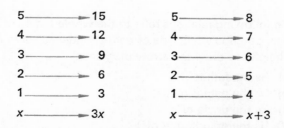

$$5 \longrightarrow 15$$
$$4 \longrightarrow 12$$
$$3 \longrightarrow 9$$
$$2 \longrightarrow 6$$
$$1 \longrightarrow 3$$
$$x \longrightarrow 3x$$

$$5 \longrightarrow 8$$
$$4 \longrightarrow 7$$
$$3 \longrightarrow 6$$
$$2 \longrightarrow 5$$
$$1 \longrightarrow 4$$
$$x \longrightarrow x+3$$

Fig. 7

Many of the relations we have seen have been ONE to ONE relations. We have seen how to represent mappings like $x \rightarrow 3x$ on two parallel number lines. See Figure 8.

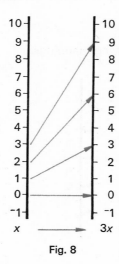

Fig. 8

We shall now study these in more detail.

2.1 Investigating mappings

On a whole page, draw two number lines that include negative numbers and then draw a mapping diagram.
Here are some suggested mappings:

$$x \rightarrow 2x, \quad x \rightarrow 3x, \quad x \rightarrow 4x, \quad x \rightarrow 1\tfrac{1}{2}x, \quad x \rightarrow 2\tfrac{1}{2}x, \quad x \rightarrow \tfrac{1}{4}x,$$

$$x \rightarrow {}^{-}x, \quad x \rightarrow {}^{-}2x,$$

$$x \rightarrow x+1, \quad x \rightarrow x+2, \quad x \rightarrow x-2, \quad x \rightarrow x-4,$$

$$x \rightarrow \frac{12}{x}, \quad x \rightarrow \frac{6}{x}, \quad x \rightarrow \frac{1}{x}.$$

Split them up amongst yourselves and build up a wall display of them. Answer the following questions:

(*a*) What is the difference between $x \rightarrow 2x$ and $x \rightarrow x+2$?

(*b*) What do you notice about all mappings like $x \rightarrow x+1$, $x \rightarrow x+2$, etc.?

(*c*) What is the connection between $x \rightarrow x+2$ and $x \rightarrow x-2$?

(*d*) What is the connection between $x \rightarrow 4x$ and $x \rightarrow \tfrac{1}{4}x$?

(*e*) In $x \rightarrow 3x$, which arrow goes straight across?

(*f*) In $x \rightarrow x+2$, which arrow goes straight across?

(g) How can you tell whether a mapping is $x \to 2x$ or $x \to 3x$?

(h) How can you tell whether a mapping is $x \to x+2$ or $x \to x+3$?

(i) How can you tell whether a mapping is $x \to 2x$ or $x \to \frac{1}{2}x$?

Exercise B

1 Identify the following mappings.

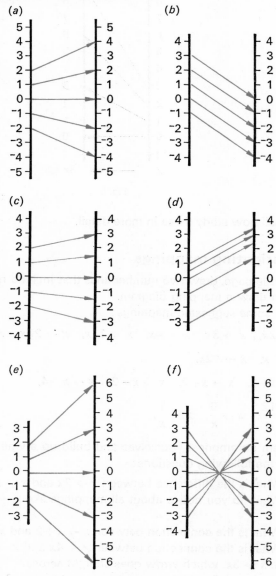

Fig. 9

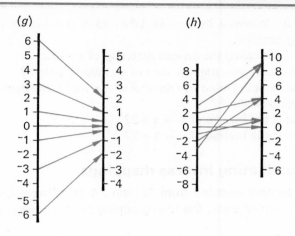

Fig. 9 *(cont.)*

3. INVERSE MAPPINGS

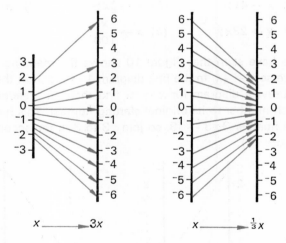

Fig. 10

What do you know about $x \rightarrow 3x$ and $x \rightarrow \frac{1}{3}x$?

What do you know about $x \rightarrow x+2$ and $x \rightarrow x-2$?

(*a*) What happens if you draw $x \rightarrow 3x$ followed by $x \rightarrow \frac{1}{3}x$?

(*b*) What happens if you draw $x \rightarrow x+2$ followed by $x \rightarrow x-2$?

What is the single mapping which has the same effect as each of the two mappings in (*a*) and in (*b*)?

109

$x \to 3x$ followed by $x \to \frac{1}{3}x$ takes each number back to its original starting position.

$x \to \frac{1}{3}x$ is called the *inverse mapping* of $x \to 3x$.

Where have you met the idea of an inverse before?

What mapping must you do after $x \to x+2$ to take each number back to its starting position?

What is the inverse of $x \to x+2$?

What is the inverse of $x \to x-2$?

3.1 Investigating inverse mappings

Draw another mapping from Section 2.1 (a different one this time). As before, display these, this time grouping them in inverse pairs.

Exercise C

1 What is the inverse mapping of each of the following mappings?

(a) $x \to x+3$; (b) $x \to x+5$; (c) $x \to x-1$;

(d) $x \to x-4$; (e) $x \to x+20$; (f) $x \to x-200$;

(g) $x \to 4x$; (h) $x \to \frac{1}{5}x$; (i) $x \to \frac{1}{9}x$;

(j) $x \to 23x$; (k) $x \to \dfrac{x}{100}$.

2 We have seen that Figure 10 shows the mapping $x \to 3x$ with its inverse $x \to \frac{1}{3}x$. In the first diagram $1 \to 3$ and in the second $3 \to 1$.

Draw a diagram for $x \to {}^{-}x$ and then on a second diagram join each number to its original starting number. This has been done for the number 3: $3 \to {}^{-}3$, so join ${}^{-}3$ to 3 in the second diagram (see Figure 11).

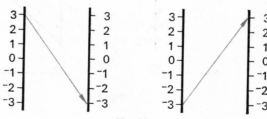

Fig. 11

What mapping is represented by the second diagram? What is the inverse mapping of $x \to {}^{-}x$?

3 Repeat Question 2 for

(a) $x \to \dfrac{1}{x}$; (b) $x \to \dfrac{12}{x}$; (c) $x \to 6-x$.

110

Interlude

CURVES OF CONSTANT WIDTH

The 50p coin is known technically as an *equilateral curved heptagon*, and it is one of a set of shapes which have an unusual, and sometimes useful, property.

The simplest member of the set is based on an equilateral triangle (see Figure 2).

Fig. 1

Fig. 2

Draw an equilateral triangle on thick card, and with compasses, centre at each vertex in turn, describe an arc on the opposite side. Cut out carefully. Pin two strips of card to a board as in Figure 3 and see if you can discover the special property of this shape.

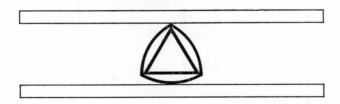

Fig. 3

Draw one of these curves round a regular pentagon.

Can you draw such a curve round a square or a regular hexagon? Can you make a general statement about this?

Why is the 50p coin one of these curves?

Other investigations

1. Find out how to drill a square hole.

2. Ask a garage for details of the Wankel engine or N.S.U. Spyder car. Try and obtain a brochure.

THE 'L' SHAPED GAME

This is a game for two players for which you will need the items shown in Figure 4.

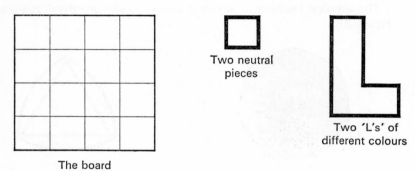

The board

Two neutral pieces

Two 'L's' of different colours

Fig. 4

Take an 'L' each, and arrange the board in the starting position shown in Figure 5.

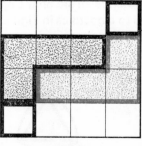

Fig. 5

Decide who is to have the first move. Each player must pick up his own 'L' and replace it in any different unoccupied position, after which he may, if he wishes, move one or other of the neutral pieces. (The 'L' piece may be reflected, rotated or translated.)

The object of the game is to manoeuvre your opponent into a position where he cannot move.

How many winning positions are there?

9. Symmetry in three dimensions

1. FILLING HOLES

You will need centimetre squared paper and scissors for the following experiments.

Experiment 1

From your squared paper cut out a rectangle which measures 3 cm by 5 cm. Draw a red arrow on the front of the rectangle (see Figure 1) and a blue arrow on the back.

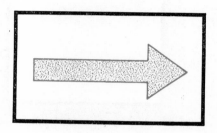

Fig. 1

In how many different ways can you fit your rectangle into the frame in Figure 2 if

    (i)   the red arrow must show;

    (ii) the blue arrow must show;

    (iii) it does not matter which arrow shows?

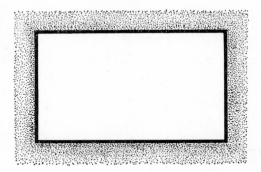

Fig. 2

Experiment 2

Cut out a square whose sides are 4 cm. Draw a red arrow on the front and a blue arrow on the back. In how many different ways can you fit your square into the frame shown in Figure 3 if

    (i)   the red arrow must show;

    (ii) it does not matter which arrow shows?

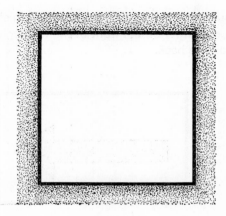

Fig. 3

(*a*) Figure 4 shows a tiling pattern with one tile missing. The tiles are white on one face and red on the other. In how many different ways can the missing tile be replaced if

    (i) it does not matter which colour shows;
   (ii) the red face of the tile must show?

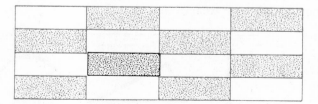

Fig. 4

(*b*) Some door handles are fitted on a rod which is a square prism and this square prism fits through a square hole in the door.

In how many ways can the door handle shown in Figure 5 be fitted to the door?

Fig. 5

(*c*) When laying a brick wall, in how many different ways can each brick be put in position?

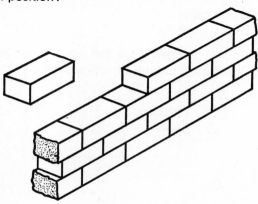

Fig. 6

115

The brick in Figure 6 can be placed in position in 4 different ways. We say that the *symmetry number* for the brick is 4.

(*d*) What is the symmetry number for the door handle in Figure 5?

(*e*) Figure 7 shows the lid of a child's postbox toy through which he 'posts' prisms of the appropriate cross-section. In how many different ways can he post each prism through its appropriate hole? What is the symmetry number for each of the prisms?

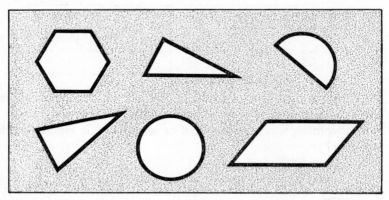

Fig. 7

Exercise A

1　In how many different ways can the following be fitted into a window frame of the appropriate shape?

(*a*)　A rectangular piece of glass;

(*b*)　a square piece of glass;

(*c*)　a semi-circular piece of glass.

2　In how many different ways can the lid be placed on

(*a*)　a rectangular cake-tin;

(*b*)　a square cake-tin;

(*c*)　a circular cake-tin?

3　In how many different ways can each of the spanners shown in Figure 8 be fitted onto the appropriate nut?

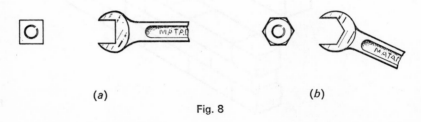

(*a*)　　　　　　　　　　　　　　　　(*b*)

Fig. 8

4 In how many ways can:

   (*a*) the key of a clockwork railway engine be fitted onto the spindle;

   (*b*) an electric lamp bulb be fitted into a lampholder?

5 Figure 9 shows the lid of another postbox toy through which prisms of the appropriate cross-section are to be posted. Name the shape of each cross-section and state the symmetry number for each prism.

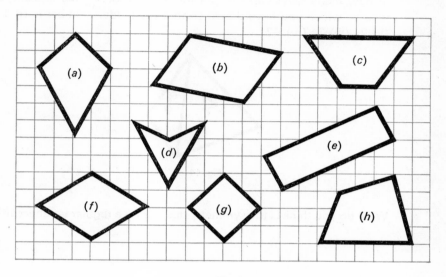

Fig. 9

6 What is the symmetry number for each of the following?

   (*a*) An unsharpened hexagonal pencil;

   (*b*) an elephant;   (*c*) a sphere;

   (*d*) a square-based pyramid;   (*e*) a shoe.

7 Place a die on paper and draw round it. In how many ways can you place the die on the square which you have drawn so that the number showing is (i) 1; (ii) 2; (iii) 3; (iv) 4; (v) 5; (vi) 6?

   In how many ways could you put the die into a box which just fits it? (See Figure 10.)

   What do you think is the symmetry number for a cube?

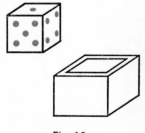

Fig. 10

117

8 (*a*) What is the symmetry number for a cuboid which measures 10 cm by 8 cm by 5 cm?

(*b*) What is the symmetry number for a cuboid which measures 10 cm by 5 cm by 5 cm?

9 Make a regular tetrahedron from card or stiff paper. Number the faces 1, 2, 3, 4. Place your tetrahedron on paper and draw round it. In how many ways can you put the tetrahedron on the equilateral triangle which you have drawn so that the hidden number is (i) 1; (ii) 2; (iii) 3; (iv) 4?

Fig. 11

What do you think is the symmetry number for a regular tetrahedron?

2. ROTATIONAL SYMMETRY

Experiment 3

Equipment: a square-based pyramid made from card or stiff paper; cocktail stick or knitting needle.

The centre of a square is the point where the diagonals intersect (see Figure 12). Use this fact to help you to prick through the centre of the base of the pyramid with the point of your compasses.

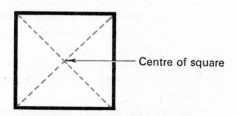

Fig. 12

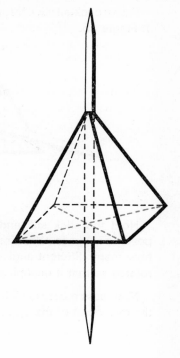

Pass a cocktail stick (or knitting needle) through the centre of the base and the vertex as shown in Figure 13.

Hold the stick still and rotate the pyramid through a quarter-turn. Does it now look the same as it did at the beginning, that is, does it occupy the same position in space?

Through how many different angles (not greater than one turn) can the pyramid be rotated so that it occupies the same position in space?

Fig. 13

Experiment 4

Equipment: a triangular prism, the triangular ends being equilateral, made from card or stiff paper (a Toblerone packet will do); cocktail stick or knitting needle.

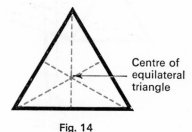

Centre of equilateral triangle

Fig. 14

The centre of an equilateral triangle is the point where the three lines of symmetry intersect (see Figure 14). Use this fact to help you to prick through the centres of the two triangular faces with the point of your compasses.

119

Pass a cocktail stick through the centres of the triangular faces as shown in Figure 15.

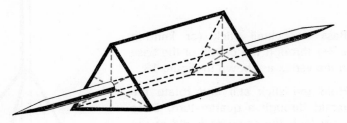

Fig. 15

Hold the stick still and rotate the prism until it occupies the same position in space. What fraction of a whole turn has been made? Through how many different angles (not greater than one turn) can the prism be rotated so that it occupies the same position in space?

Now pass a cocktail stick through the centre of a rectangular face and the mid-point of the opposite edge as shown in Figure 16.

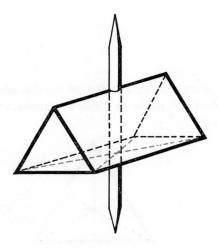

Fig. 16

Hold the stick still and rotate the prism until it occupies the same position in space. What fraction of a whole turn has been made?

Through how many angles (not greater than one turn) can the prism be rotated so that it occupies the same position in space?

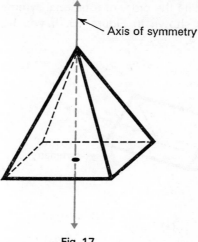

Fig. 17

In Experiment 3, you found that the pyramid in Figure 17 can be mapped onto itself in four different ways by rotation about the red axis. We therefore say that the pyramid has *rotational symmetry of order 4* about this axis, which is called an *axis of symmetry*.

What is the symmetry number for a square-based pyramid?

If a three-dimensional figure can be fitted in its appropriate hole in more than one way, its symmetry number must be greater than 1. It must then have rotational symmetry about one or more axes.

A solid with no rotational symmetry and a symmetry number of 1 (see Figure 18), can be mapped onto itself by a rotation through one whole turn about *any* axis which we care to choose.

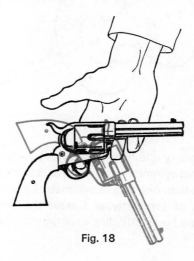

Fig. 18

(*a*) (i) State the order of rotational symmetry of the prism about each of the axes shown in Figure 19. If you have difficulty, look again at Experiment 4.

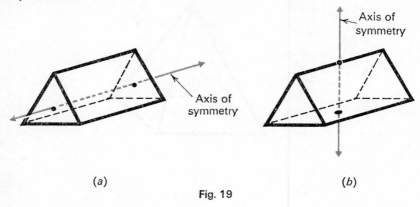

(*a*)   (*b*)

Fig. 19

(ii) The prism has two other axes of symmetry. Use your prism and cocktail stick to try to find them. What is the order of rotational sym-metry about each of these axes?

(iii) What is the symmetry number for the prism? Is it greater than 1?

(*b*) The symmetry number for the door handle in Figure 5 is 4. What is the order of rotational symmetry about the axis shown in Figure 20? Do you think that the handle has more than one axis of symmetry?

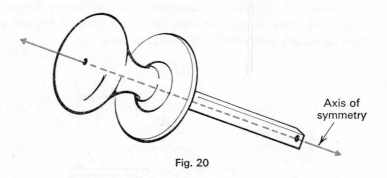

Fig. 20

(*c*) The symmetry number for the brick in Figure 6 is also 4. What is the order of rotational symmetry about the axis shown in Figure 21? Does the brick have more than one axis of symmetry? If so, draw a diagram to show any other axes of symmetry and state the corresponding order(s) of symmetry. (If you have difficulty, experiment with a model and a cocktail stick.)

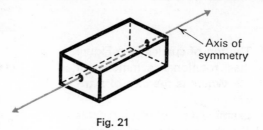

Fig. 21

Exercise B

For this exercise you will need models made from card, a cocktail stick and a pack of cards.

1   State the order of rotational symmetry about each of the axes shown in Figure 22. If you have difficulty, use your models and cocktail stick.

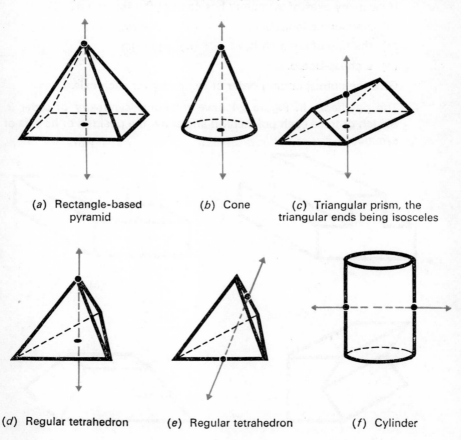

(a) Rectangle-based   (b) Cone   (c) Triangular prism, the
       pyramid   triangular ends being isosceles

(d) Regular tetrahedron   (e) Regular tetrahedron   (f) Cylinder

Fig. 22

2 (*a*) The ten of spades (see Figure 23) has rotational symmetry of order 2. Where is the axis of symmetry?

(*b*) Examine a set of playing cards and list the members of this set which have rotational symmetry of order 2.

Fig. 23

3 How many axes of symmetry has each of the following?
   (*a*) An electric lamp bulb;   (*b*) a drawing pin;
   (*c*) the tray of a match box;   (*d*) a jam-jar;
   (*e*) a chess-board.

   Give the corresponding order of symmetry for each axis.

4 The polyhedra in Figure 24 have rotational symmetry of order 2. Sketch or trace each polyhedron and show the position of its axis of symmetry.

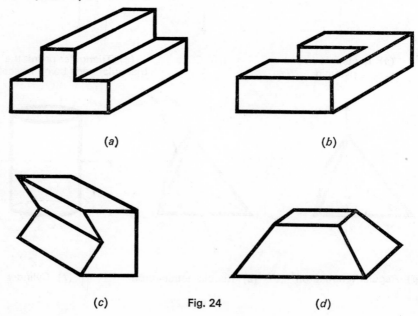

(*a*)   (*b*)

(*c*)   Fig. 24   (*d*)

5 Use a cube and cocktail stick to find the order of rotational symmetry about each of the axes shown in Figure 25.

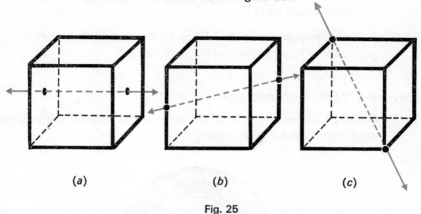

(a)   (b)   (c)

Fig. 25

6 Use a regular octahedron and cocktail stick to find the order of rotational symmetry about each of the axes shown in Figure 26.

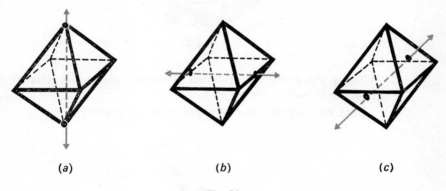

(a)   (b)   (c)

Fig. 26

Class projects

7 Collect some objects in everyday use which have rotational symmetry. State the number of axes of symmetry which each possesses and the order about each axis. Make a classroom display.

8 How many axes of symmetry has

   (a) a cube;
   (b) a regular tetrahedron;
   (c) a regular octahedron?

Use card or thick paper and cocktail sticks or knitting needles to make a set of models showing these axes. Find the order of rotational symmetry about each axis.

9 Collect photographs of buildings having interesting features with rotational symmetry and make a wall display.

Exercise C (Miscellaneous)

1 Figure 27 shows a man removing a car wheel. In how many different ways can he put it back again?

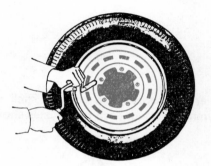

Fig. 27

2 What is the order of rotational symmetry about the axis of the propeller shown in Figure 28?

Does the propeller have any planes of symmetry?

Fig. 28

126

3   Figure 29 shows three tiling patterns. All the tiles are red on one face and white on the other. For each of the missing tiles, say which colour face should show and in how many different ways it can be replaced.

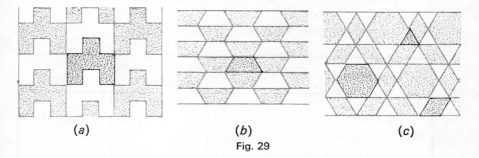

(*a*)   (*b*)   (*c*)

Fig. 29

4   Figure 30 shows a square-based right pyramid.

(*a*) What is the symmetry number?

(*b*) Through what point of the base does the axis of symmetry pass?

(*c*) State the number of planes of symmetry.

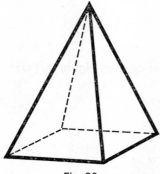

Fig. 30

Fig. 31

5   Make a regular tetrahedron from stiff white paper.

(*a*) What is the symmetry number for a regular tetrahedron? (Consider each vertex in turn being fitted into the hole shown in Figure 31.)

(*b*) How many planes and axes of symmetry has it?

(*c*) Colour one of the faces red. The tetrahedron now has three white faces and one red face. How many planes and axes of symmetry has it?

(*d*) Colour another face blue. The tetrahedron now has two white faces, one red face and one blue face.

127

Stand it on one of its white faces; then toss it up until it again comes to rest on one of its white faces. By examining the colours of the other faces, can you tell whether it is standing on the same white face as before or not?

How many planes and axes of symmetry has it now?

6 Copy and complete the following table.

Polyhedron	Number of planes of symmetry	Number of axes of symmetry	Symmetry number
Triangular prism (regular)			
Hexagonal prism (regular)			
Cylinder			
Regular tetrahedron			
Cube			
Regular octahedron			

Summary

A solid can have:

(a) *axes of rotational symmetry*—spearing (see Figure 32 (a));

Fig. 32 (a)

(*b*) *planes of symmetry*—chopping (see Figure 32 (*b*)).

Fig. 32 (*b*)

The *symmetry number* is the number of ways in which a solid can be placed in a hole of the same shape and size (see Figure 33).

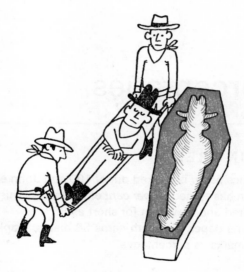

Fig. 33

10. Percentages

1. PER HUNDRED

A Mathematics paper is marked out of 100 and John earns 80 marks. We say that John has earned 80 *per cent* of the marks. This *percentage* means 80 per hundred and is written for short as 80%.

On the same paper, Elizabeth earns 88 marks, Frank 74 and Anne 63. Write these marks as percentages.

A second paper is marked out of 50 ; John earns 30 marks, Elizabeth 45, Frank 40 and Anne 25.

John earns $\frac{30}{50}$ of the marks for this paper. Write this fraction so that the bottom number is 100. Now write John's mark as a percentage.

Use Figure 1 to help you to write the other three marks as percentages.

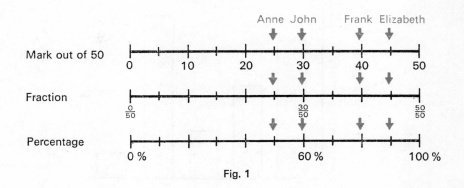

Fig. 1

In order to write a fraction as a percentage, we first find an equivalent fraction with a bottom number of 100. For example,

$$\frac{30}{50} = \frac{30 \times 2}{50 \times 2} = \frac{60}{100} = 60\%.$$

Exercise A

1 Copy and complete:

(a) $\frac{9}{10} = \frac{90}{100} = \quad$ %;   (b) $\frac{2}{5} = \frac{}{100} = \quad$ %;

(c) $\frac{1}{4} = \frac{}{100} = \quad$ %;   (d) $\frac{1}{25} = \frac{}{100} = \quad$ %;

(e) $\frac{3}{20} = \frac{}{100} = \quad$ %;   (f) $\frac{1}{2} = \frac{}{100} = \quad$ %.

2 In a Geography examination, the following marks are obtained out of a total of 200:

Anne   80,

Elizabeth   144,

John   124,

Frank   135.

Write these marks as percentages.

3 (a) What does 100% mean? Write a sentence using it sensibly.
(b) Is it possible to give a meaning to 200%? Give a reason for your answer.

4 Write the following fractions as percentages:

(a) $\frac{19}{100}$; (b) $\frac{3}{4}$; (c) $\frac{7}{10}$; (d) $\frac{1}{5}$; (e) $\frac{2}{1}$; (f) $\frac{400}{500}$;

(g) $\frac{11}{20}$; (h) $\frac{49}{50}$; (i) $\frac{5}{2}$; (j) $\frac{66}{150}$; (k) $\frac{1}{8}$; (l) $\frac{3}{2}$.

131

5   Figure 2 shows how a form comes to school.

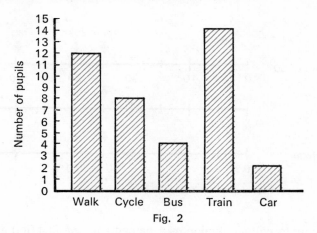

Fig. 2

(*a*) How many pupils are there in the form?
(*b*) How many of the form walk to school? What fraction of the form is this? Write this fraction as a percentage.
(*c*) What percentage of the form come to school by

        (i) bus;   (ii) train;   (iii) car?

6   Copy and complete:

(*a*) $0·25 = \frac{25}{100} = $ %;   (*b*) $0·75 = \frac{}{100} = $ %;

(*c*) $0·45 = \frac{}{100} = $ %;   (*d*) $0·73 = \frac{}{100} = $ %;

(*e*) $0·3 = \frac{}{10} = \frac{}{100} = $ %;   (*f*) $0·8 = \frac{}{10} = \frac{}{100} = $ %;

(*g*) $0·5 = \frac{}{10} = \frac{}{100} = $ %;   (*h*) $1·5 = \frac{}{10} = \frac{}{100} = $ %.

7   In Figure 3, the number line between 0 and 1 is marked in three equivalent ways. What is the relation between: (*a*) any fraction and the corresponding percentage; (*b*) any decimal and the corresponding percentage?

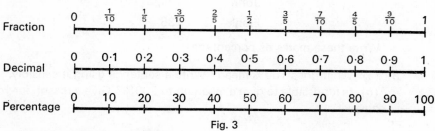

Fig. 3

8   What percentage is:

(*a*) 1p of £1;   (*b*) 1 cm of 1 m;   (*c*) 1 m of 1 km;

(*d*) 20 g of 1 kg;   (*e*) 120 m of 1 km;   (*f*) 50p of £2?

2. FROM PERCENTAGE TO FRACTION

What does 75% mean? Write this as a fraction so that the bottom number is 100.

In a History examination, Anne obtained 75%. What fraction of the total marks did she earn? Write this fraction in its simplest form.

Exercise B

1 Write the following percentages as fractions in their simplest form:
   (a) 50%; (b) 1%;   (c) 25%; (d) 10%; (e) 40%;
   (f) 5%;   (g) 45%;   (h) 7%;   (i) 12%; (j) 100%;
   (k) 0·5%; (l) 2·5%; (m) 12·5%; (n) 150%; (o) 37·5%;
   (p) 0·8%; (q) 62·5%; (r) $33\frac{1}{3}$%; (s) $66\frac{2}{3}$%; (t) 125%.

2 A rope shrinks 0·6% when wetted. What fraction is this?

3 On Friday, 20% of a class was absent. What fraction is this? What fraction of the pupils was present? What percentage of the pupils was present?

4 (a) If 13% is wasted, what % is saved?
   (b) If 69% pass, what % fail?

5 A man spends 12% of his income on rent and 58% on household expenses. What percentage remains?

3. USING PERCENTAGES

Copy and complete the following examples.

Example 1

Frank received 40% in a test which was marked out of 20. How many marks did he get?

Frank received 40% $= \frac{}{100}$ of the total marks awarded,

and so he was given $\frac{40}{100}$ of 20 marks $= \frac{40}{100} \times 20$ marks $=$ marks.

Example 2

Mr Jones pays $7\frac{1}{2}$% interest on a loan of £4. How much interest does he pay?

Mr Jones paid $7\frac{1}{2}$% $= \frac{}{100}$ of the loan,

and so he paid $\frac{7\frac{1}{2}}{100}$ of £4 $= \frac{7\frac{1}{2}}{100}$ of 400p $=$ p.

Exercise C

1 Find the number of marks which Frank would have received if he was awarded:

   (a) 85% on a paper marked out of 100;

   (b) 60% on a paper marked out of 200;

   (c) 30% on a paper marked out of 120.

2 Find the values of:

   (a) 10% of £1;   (b) 20% of £300;

   (c) 75% of 240 kg;   (d) 30% of 80 marks;

   (e) 6% of 45 m;   (f) 5% of 15 cm.

3 In a school of 800 pupils, 11% are prefects. How many prefects are there?

4 I pay 8% interest on a loan of £250. How much interest do I pay?

5 In a school of 700 pupils, 69% have had measles. How many is this? How many have not had measles?

6 Would you prefer to have 75% of £420 or 35% of £880? Show your working.

7 Mr Smith pays 12% of his salary into a pension fund. How much does he pay if his salary is £825? How much extra will he have to pay if his salary is increased to £900?

8

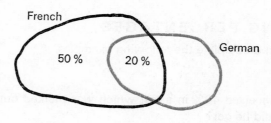

Fig. 4

All the pupils in a school learn French or German or both. 50% learn French only and 20% learn both (see Figure 4). What percentage of the pupils learns German only? There are 750 pupils in the school. How many learn German only?

9 A salesman receives 12½% commission on his sales. What is his commission for selling a television set for £120?

4. MORE PERCENTAGES

Copy and complete the following examples.

Example 3

Jimmy's wages have just been increased by 13%. If he was earning £600 per year, how much is he earning now?

A 13% increase means that Jimmy now receives an extra 13% of £600.

$$13\% = \frac{}{100},$$

and so the increase is $\frac{13}{100}$ of £600 = £   .

Jimmy now earns £600 + £78 = £   .

Example 4

In January 1968 I bought a car for £500 and a year later its value had decreased by 25%. What was it worth in January 1969?

A 25% decrease means that the value of the car has decreased by 25% of £500.

$$25\% = \frac{}{100},$$

and so the decrease is $\frac{25}{100}$ of £500 = £   .

The value of the car in January 1969 is £500 − £   = £   .

Exercise D

1   A girl's pocket money is increased by 25%. If it was 12p, how much is it now?

2   I used to be able to type at 60 words per minute, but I am out of practice and my speed has dropped by 5%. What is my present speed?

3   If I buy a house for £5000 and I gain 30% when I sell it, how much do I get for the house?

4   A nylon rope 50 m long will stretch 1 m. What percentage is this? How far would you expect 180 m of the same rope to stretch?

5   At an annual sale, the prices of all articles are reduced by 10%. What is the sale price of articles which normally cost (*a*) £5; (*b*) £2; (*c*) 60p; (*d*) £120?

6   A car costs £1000 when new. Its value decreases by 25% in the first year and by 12% of its value at the beginning of the year in the second year. Find the value of the car (*a*) after 1 year; (*b*) after 2 years.

Exercise E (Miscellaneous)

1

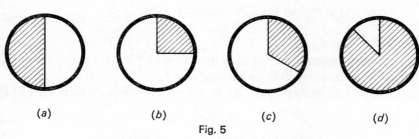

(a)	*(b)*	*(c)*	*(d)*

Fig. 5

What percentage of each circle in Figure 5 is shaded red?
What percentage of each circle is unshaded?

2   Copy and complete the following:

(*a*) 50p is   % of £1 ;   (*b*) 20p is   % of 80p ;

(*c*) 50 m is   % of 2 km ;   (*d*) 30 g is   % of 4 kg ;

(*e*) £45 is   % of £500 ;   (*f*) £30 is   % of £90.

3   A boy earns 120 marks out of 180. What percentage is this? If the pass mark is 45%, what is the lowest mark for passing?

4   There are 4360 candidates for an examination, and 45% fail. How many candidates pass?

5   The pie chart in Figure 6 shows how a family spent their total income last month. What percentage of their income was spent on (*a*) food; (*b*) heating; (*c*) clothing; (*d*) rent?

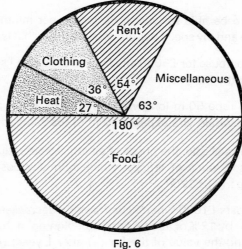

Fig. 6

6   What percentage of the lesson time in your form is spent on Mathematics?

7   My coal merchant gives a discount of 5% on all bills paid within 7 days. How much discount can I get on a bill for £4·40?

8   Peter buys a bicycle for £20 and pays a deposit of 15%. How much money does he still owe?

9   Gunmetal contains 9 times as much copper as tin. Find the percentage of copper in the gunmetal.

10   Chalk contains calcium, carbon and oxygen in the ratio 10 to 3 to 12. Find the percentage of carbon in the chalk.

11   Gunpowder is made from 75% nitre, 15% charcoal and 10% sulphur. Find the amount of (*a*) nitre, (*b*) charcoal and (*c*) sulphur in 4 kg of gunpowder.

12   The duty on an article is 10% of its value. If the duty is £2, find the value of the article.

13   Anne buys a book for £1·50 and sells it at a loss of 12%. How much does she get for it?

14   John earns £900 per year. How much will he earn if he is given a rise of $7\frac{1}{2}$%?

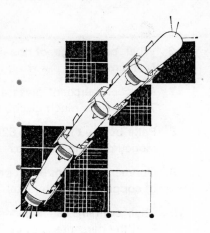

11. Graphical interpretation

1. A GRAPHICAL READY RECKONER

Have you noticed how, when a petrol pump attendant is filling a car with petrol, both the amount and the cost of the petrol are often recorded automatically on dials on the pump?

(a) How does this help an attendant who is asked for each of the following?

    (i) '20 litres of petrol please'.
    (ii) '80p worth of petrol please'.

(b) Suppose 1 litre of petrol costs 10p.

    (i) How much would 10 litres of petrol cost?
    (ii) How much would 20 litres of petrol cost?
    (iii) How much petrol would a motorist get for 100p?

This kind of information can be represented by ordered pairs of numbers; for example:

    (10, 100) could represent '10 litres of petrol, cost 100p',

    (20, 200) could represent '20 litres of petrol, cost 200p'.

Find the cost of 5 litres of petrol and complete the ordered pair (5,   ).
Figure 1 shows the ordered pairs representing information, plotted on graph paper.

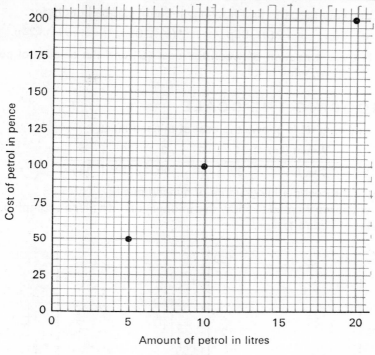

Fig. 1

What do you notice about the points plotted?

Make a copy of Figure 1 and join the points with a ruler.

(*c*) Use your graph to find the cost of

(i) 12 litres; (ii) $7\frac{1}{2}$ litres; (iii) $16\frac{1}{2}$ litres.

Does (0, 0) have a meaning? Do *all* the points on the line have a meaning? Why? How long can we make the line?

If a garage were to refuse to sell fractions of a litre, would every point on the line have a meaning then?

Exercise A

1 (*a*) Why is there a different scale along each axis in Figure 1 ?

(*b*) What *is* the same about the scales along the two axes? Why?

(*c*) On the axis across the page, what does 2 mm represent?

(*d*) On the axis up the page, what does 2 mm represent?

2 Use your graph to find or estimate the cost of the following amounts of petrol:

(*a*) 9 litres; (*b*) $2\frac{1}{2}$ litres; (*c*) $12\frac{1}{2}$ litres.

3   Use your graph to find how much petrol can be bought for:

  (a) 80p;   (b) 55p;   (c) 185p;   (d) $112\frac{1}{2}$p.

4   Is there a relation between the cost (C) and the amount of petrol (L)? If so, what is it?

2.   CHOOSING THE SCALE

The following table shows the cost of minced meat.

Weight (kg)	1	2	3	4	5
Cost (p)	30	60	90	120	150

What is the cost per kilogramme of minced meat?

Suppose we wanted to show this information on a piece of graph paper the size of Figure 1.

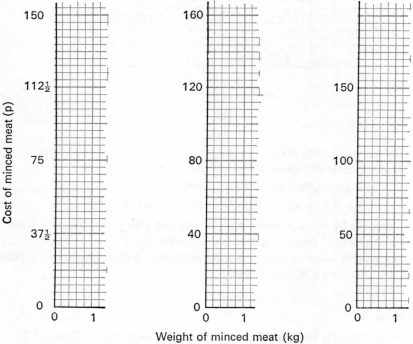

Weight of minced meat (kg)

Fig. 2

Figure 2 shows three pupils' attempts at choosing a scale. Obviously, they all came to the same decision about the scale across the page. What was this?

Discuss the three different scales up the page. What does 2 mm represent on each one? Which scale would you choose to work on and why?

140

Exercise B

1 The following tables do not need explaining. For each one, discuss what scales *you* would use on *your* graph paper if you were asked to represent the information graphically. Having decided, then plot the points. (Remember that the scale on each axis must be marked out evenly.)

(*a*)

Weight of beef (kg)	1	2	3	4	5
Cost (p)	50	100	150	200	250

(*b*)

Amount of potatoes (kg)	1	2	3	5	10
Cost (p)	5	10	15	25	50

(*c*)

Time taken (h)	1	2	3	4	5	6	7	8
Distance travelled (km)	60	120	180	240	300	360	420	480

(*d*)

Distance travelled (km)	0	50	100	200	400	600
Petrol left in tank (litres)	50	46	42	34	18	2

2 Take the cost of minced meat as 30p a kilogramme and complete the following table:

Weight (kg)	1	2	3	4
Cost (p)				

Plot this information on graph paper and answer the following questions.

(*a*) If you draw a straight line through the points, will every point on the line have a meaning?
(*b*) How much meat could be bought for 64p, 48p, 72p, 75p, 115p?
(*c*) What is the cost of 2·5 kg, 3·4 kg, 1·7 kg, 3·75 kg?
(*d*) What is the relation between the cost and the weight?

3 I make a journey of 240 km in my car and average 10 km to each litre of petrol. I start with 30 litres of petrol in the tank. The following table describes the relation between the distance travelled and the petrol left.

Distance travelled (km)	0	30	60	90	120	150	180	210	240
Petrol left (litres)	30	27	24	21	18	15	12	9	6

Show this information on a coordinate diagram. Is it reasonable to join the points by a straight line?

141

(*a*) How much petrol was left after I had travelled (i) 70 km, (ii) 165 km?

(*b*) How far had I gone when there were (i) 16 litres, (ii) 7·5 litres left?

(*c*) *Calculate* how much further I could have travelled before running out of petrol. How could you find this information from your graph?

4 Christmas cards cost 25p a box. Complete the following ordered pairs which show (number of boxes, cost in pence):

$$(1, \ ); \ (2, \ ); \ (3, \ ); \ (4, \ ).$$

Plot these points on graph paper. Is it reasonable to join them up with a straight line if

(i) only whole boxes can be purchased;
(ii) boxes contain 10 cards each and the shop will split them up.

How could we find the cost of 5 boxes *without* doing any arithmetic?

3. LINEAR RELATIONS

In the last two sections we have looked at relations whose graphs were straight lines. Such relations are called *linear relations*.

3.1 Graphs and how to use them

Example 1

When buying Christmas cards with your name and address printed on them, the catalogue quotes a number of prices for different quantities. The price is usually

(i) a basic charge for the printing block, plus
(ii) a fixed amount for each card.

Figure 3 shows the graph of the relation between the number of cards (*x*) and the price (*y*) for two different cards *A* and *B*.

(*a*) Use the graph to find the cost of (i) 10, (ii) 20, (iii) 25, (iv) 42 of each card.

(*b*) Which is the more expensive card?

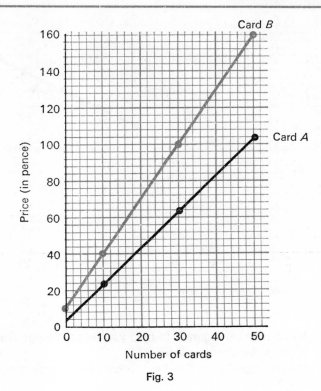

Fig. 3

(c) The basic charge for card *A* is 4p. What is the basic charge for card *B*?

(d) The cost of a single card *A* (after paying the basic charge) is 2p. What is the cost of a single card *B*?

(e) Would the graph for an even more expensive card be more or less steep than the lines in Figure 3?

(f) Does every point on the line have a meaning?

(g) Would it be reasonable to extend the lines in either direction?

Example 2

The price of ladders of different lengths is shown in the following table:

Number of rungs (x)	10	12	14	16	18	20
Price of ladder (y pounds)	7	8	9	10	11	12

Figure 4 (over page) represents this information graphically.

The cost consists of (i) a basic charge, plus (ii) a charge per rung.

143

Graphical interpretation

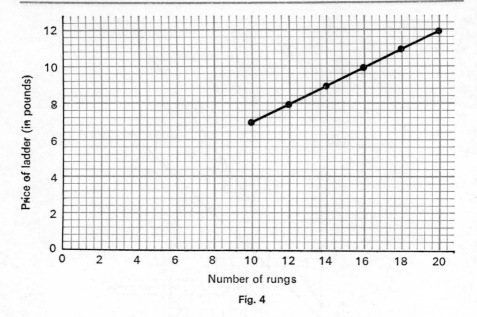

Fig. 4

(*a*) Use a ruler on Figure 4 to help you find the basic charge.

(*b*) What is the charge per rung?

(*c*) Do any points on the line (other than those marked) have a meaning?

(*d*) Is it reasonable to extend the line in either direction?

(*e*) How much would a 7-rung ladder cost?

(*f*) What is the relation between x and y?

Exercise C

In this exercise remember to label your axes and to choose the scales along them carefully.

1 Here are the playing times for various lengths of recording tape moving at 25 cm/s.

Tape length (x m)	240	360	480	720	960
Playing time (y min)	16	24	32	48	64

(*a*) Represent this information on a coordinate diagram.

(*b*) Is the relation between x and y linear?

(*c*) If you wanted to record a piece of music lasting 20 minutes, what would be the shortest length of tape which would do?

(*d*) How long would 540 m of tape play?

144

2 Hit-it-Hard and Company, a table tennis bat hiring firm, make a basic charge of 3p for loaning out a bat, and on top of that they charge $\frac{1}{2}$p per day.

(*a*) Complete the following table:

Number of days	1	2	3	4	5	7	10	n
Charge (in pence)	$3\frac{1}{2}$	4	$4\frac{1}{2}$					

(*b*) If C pence is the charge for n days, write down a relation connecting C and n.

(*c*) Draw the graph of the relation with values of n across the page and values of C up the page. (Take 1 cm to represent 1p *and* 1 day.)

(*d*) Use the graph to find how long you could have a bat for a charge of (i) 9p, (ii) $10\frac{1}{2}$p.

3 A rocket launches a spacecraft on the first stage of its journey, which lasts ten minutes. At blast-off the rocket has 20 000 litres of fuel, but it uses it at a steady rate of 2000 litres per minute.

Draw a graph to show this relation (see table).

Number of litres of fuel in tank	20 000	18 000	16 000	12 000	8000	4000	0
Number of minutes since 'blast-off'	0	1	2	4	6	8	10

From your graph find how long after 'blast-off' there are 19 500 litres remaining. How much fuel is left after $8\frac{1}{2}$ minutes?

4 In a science experiment, a piece of elastic is fixed at one end and different weights are hung from the other end. The length of the elastic is measured each time a weight is hung on it (see Figure 5).
The measurements are shown in this table:

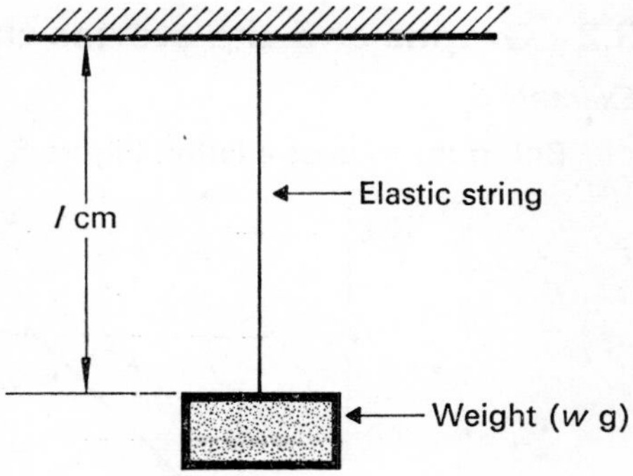

Fig. 5

Weight (w g)	0	5	10	15	20	25	30
Length of elastic (l cm)	30·2	41·7	50·1	58·5	71·0	80·4	90·8

(*a*) Plot these results on graph paper. Why don't the points lie on an exact straight line?

(*b*) Approximately what length would you expect the elastic to be if the weight was:

(i) 8 g;   (ii) 11 g;   (iii) 26 g;   (iv) 32 g?

(*c*) Is it reasonable to draw a straight line through some of the points you have plotted? Draw the best line you can.

(*d*) Approximately what weight will produce an *increase in length* of the elastic of:

(i) 10 cm;   (ii) 20 cm;   (iii) 30 cm?

(*e*) Find an approximate relation between the length of the elastic and the weight.

Try the experiment for yourselves and record and graph your own results.

5 When a polygon has *n* sides, the sum, *S*, of all the interior angles is $2n - 4$ right-angles.

(*a*) Copy and complete the following table:

n	S
3	
6	
9	14
12	

(*b*) Represent the information in this table on a graph.

(*c*) Use the points you have plotted to find the value of *S* when a polygon has:

(i) 4 sides;   (ii) 8 sides;   (iii) 10 sides.

3.2 Graphs and the stories they tell

Example 3

Bob goes to post a letter. Figure 6 shows his progress.

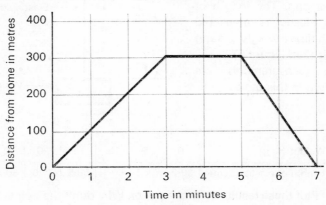

Fig. 6

(*a*) How far did he go in the first minute?

(*b*) How far did he travel in (i) the second minute, (ii) the third minute?

(*c*) Do you think he walked or ran?

(*d*) Did he keep a steady pace during the first three minutes?

(*e*) What does the horizontal part of the graph show?

(*f*) Did the journey to or from the post box take the longest?

Example 4

Gillian leaves home to walk to school (1000 m away) at a steady rate of 100 metres every minute.

How far will she have walked after (i) 2 minutes, (ii) 5 minutes?

Figure 7 shows the start of her journey. Copy it onto graph paper but use a larger scale.

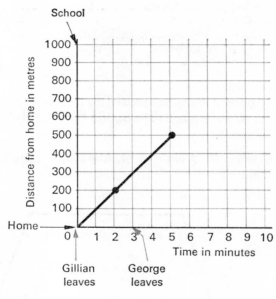

Fig. 7

(*a*) If Gillian continues to walk at the same rate, extend the graph and find how long it takes her to get to school.

(*b*) Her brother George leaves home three minutes after her and cycles steadily at 400 metres every minute. On the same figure, show his journey. What do you find? Can you explain what happens?

(*c*) How long does it take George to catch up Gillian?

(*d*) How long after George does Gillian arrive at school?

147

Exercise D

1 Figure 8 shows the sad story of a boy trying to catch a bus. Describe what you think happened.

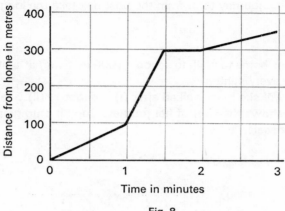

Fig. 8

If he had gone at the same speed all the time, what would that speed have been? (Use the graph to help you.) Draw the line that represents this steady speed.

2 A bath is being filled with water. Make up a story to explain the graph in Figure 9.

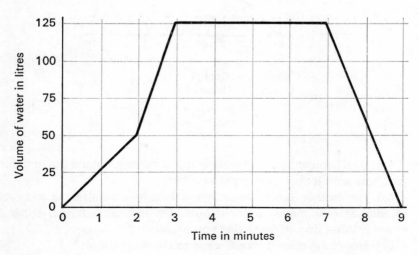

Fig. 9

3 Make up a story, giving as much detail as you can, to explain the graph in Figure 10.

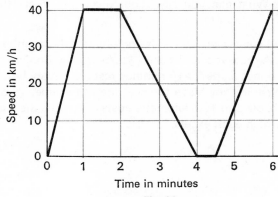

Fig. 10

4 Draw the graph representing a person who ran at 200 metres per minute for $2\frac{1}{2}$ minutes, had a rest for $\frac{1}{2}$ minute and then turned back and walked home at 150 metres per minute.

5 A man cycled from town *A* to town *B*, a distance of 3 kilometres in 10 minutes. He left his cycle for repair, spending 10 minutes in the town and then walked home to *A* in $\frac{1}{2}$ hour. Represent this by a graph.

6 An Electricity Board charges for electricity in the following way:

       the first 60 units cost 3p each,

       the next 60 units cost 2p each,

       all units after the first 120 units cost 1p each.

(*a*) What will be the cost of 12, 24, 30, 48, 60 units?

(*b*) 90 units cost $(60 \times 3) + (30 \times 2) = 180 + 60 = 240$p. What will be the cost of 80, 100, 120 units?

(*c*) Use your last answer to (*b*) to find the cost of 140 units.

(*d*) Draw a graph giving the number of units of electricity used, from 0 to 400, across the page. What do you need to know before you can work out the scale for the cost?

(*e*) Use your graph to estimate the cost of:

(i) 45 units; (ii) 92 units; (iii) 240 units; (iv) 378 units.

7 A cyclist cycles at 18 km/h in travelling from Preston to Sheffield, a distance of 108 km. If he leaves Preston at 9 a.m., what time will he reach Sheffield, assuming he does not stop on the way? How far will the cyclist be from Preston at 10 a.m., 11 a.m., 12 noon, 1 p.m., 2 p.m., 3 p.m.?

Meanwhile, a car leaves Sheffield at midday and travels towards Preston at 45 km/h. Find its distance from Sheffield at hourly intervals.

Represent both sets of information on the same coordinate diagram. What can you say about the point where the two lines meet?

8 Using the same axes, draw the graphs which describe the journey made by Arthur who walks at $3\frac{1}{2}$ km/h, and by Benjamin who walks at 4 km/h, but stops for 15 minutes rest after every hour of walking. Assuming that they leave town at the same time, who arrives first at the 4th, 8th and 12th kilometre posts? Describe the sort of walking race at which each excels.

12. Number patterns

1. PASCAL'S TRIANGLE

A boy enters the maze shown above, at *A*, and wants to know how many different routes there are to the fountain.

At *A* he can go either to the left or to the right. If we assume that he always goes further into the maze, then at *B* or *C* he also goes left or right.

So there are two possible routes to *E*:

$$A \to B \to E \quad \text{and} \quad A \to C \to E.$$

Copy Figure 1 and fill in the number of possible different routes to each point.

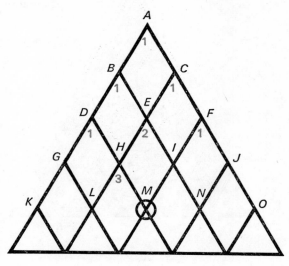

Fig. 1

Can you say how many different routes there are to the fountain?

Copy the following triangle of numbers and see if you can find out how each row is determined from the previous one.

Add several more rows.

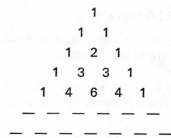

This triangle of numbers is called *Pascal's Triangle*, after a famous French mathematician. It contains many interesting number patterns.

Can you find the following number sequences in the triangle?

(*a*) 1, 2, 3, 4, 5, ...;
(*b*) 1, 3, 6, 10, 15, ...

The first set of numbers is the set of counting numbers. What is the second set called?

Exercise A

1   Add all the numbers in each row of Pascal's triangle.

$$1 \qquad = 1$$
$$1+1 \quad = 2$$
$$1+2+1 \quad = 4$$
$$1+3+3+1 = 8 \quad \text{and so on.}$$

Without adding them up, say what the sum of the numbers in the following rows will be:

    (*a*) 10th;   (*b*) 12th;   (*c*) 14th;   (*d*) *n*th.

2

$$11^1 = \quad 11$$
$$11^2 = \quad 121$$
$$11^3 = 1331$$

Continue this number pattern and explain why it eventually fails to agree with Pascal's triangle.

3   On a large sheet of paper write out the numbers of Pascal's triangle up to at least row 15.

    Take a sheet of squared paper and turn it cornerwise. Imagine the numbers of Pascal's triangle written in the small squares, as shown in Figure 2. Do not fill in the actual numbers, just put a red dot if the number is even, a black dot if the number is odd (see Figure 3).

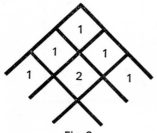

Fig. 2

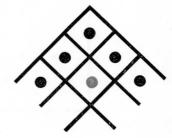

Fig. 3

Continue up to at least row fifteen. Describe the pattern you find.

    Now try putting a red dot if the number is divisible by 3, a black dot if it is not.

4   In the 8th row of Pascal's triangle, the second number, 7, is a factor of all the other numbers in that row excluding the 1's at either end. Is this true for all rows?

    What sort of a number must the second number be for this to be true?

6   SMD

5 All numbers in row 4 of Pascal's triangle are odd. Write down the numbers of other rows consisting entirely of odd numbers—your diagram for Question 3 will help.

What do you notice?

Will all the numbers in row 256 be odd?

6 Re-write Pascal's triangle as shown in Figure 4 with the first column of 1's vertical. Add the numbers in the diagonals and write the answer at the side. These are the numbers you get:

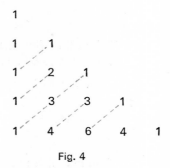

1, 1, 2, 3, 5, 8, ...

Can you guess the next number?
What would be (a) the 8th; (b) the 10th number?

Fig. 4

Experiment 1

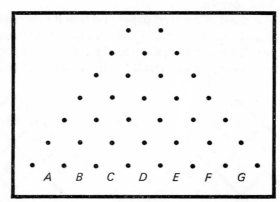

Fig. 5

For this experiment you will need a square of plywood approximately 30 cm by 30 cm, nails and several marbles.

Hammer the nails into the wood in the triangle pattern shown in Figure 5. Adjust the gaps so that your marbles will just pass between any two nails.

Drop a marble in at the top 100 times and record which box it ends up in: A, B, C, D, E, F or G. What do you find?

Which box is entered least often? Is this what you would expect? (Look back at the maze problem.)

154

2. THE FIBONACCI SEQUENCE

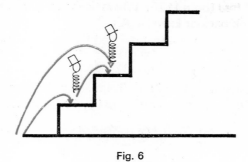

Fig. 6

If you can run upstairs one step or two steps at a time, in how many different ways can you get to each stair?

First step—Just 1 way

Second step—2 ways

Third step—3 ways

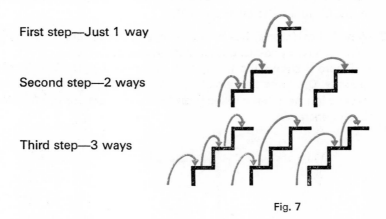

Fig. 7

Draw diagrams of your own for 4 steps and for 5 steps.

Draw a staircase with 6 steps and fill in the number of different ways to each step (see Figure 8).

You will obtain a sequence of numbers

$$1, 2, 3, 5, \ldots.$$

Each term of this sequence has a certain connection with some of the terms immediately before it. Can you spot the connection?

Fig. 8

6-2

1, 2, 3, 5, ...

This sequence of numbers is called the *Fibonacci sequence* after Leonardo Fibonacci of Pisa (born 1175). Where have you come across this sequence before? (Look back at Exercise A.)

Exercise B

1 Suppose you had a pile of fivepenny and tenpenny pieces; in how many ways could you make up 5p, 10p, 15p, ...?

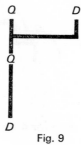

Amount		Number of ways
5p	Ⓕ	1
10p	Ⓕ Ⓕ or Ⓣ	2
15p	Ⓕ Ⓕ Ⓕ or Ⓣ Ⓕ or Ⓕ Ⓣ	3

Guess how many ways you could make up 20p, then see if you are right. Continue the table up to 30p.

2 A male bee (drone) has only one parent, the queen. A queen, however, has two parents, a queen and a drone.

Figure 9 shows the family tree of a male bee back to its grandparents. Continue the family tree back through six more generations (assuming no intermarriage!) and note the number of ancestors in each generation.

Q   D

Q

D

Fig. 9

3 Write out the first 15 terms of the Fibonacci sequence starting 1, 1, 2, and number the terms from 1 to 15 (see below).

1 2 3 4 5 6 7 8 9 10 11 12 13 14 15
1 1 ② ③ ⟨5⟩ ⑧ 13 21⃞

Mark with a circle all the Fibonacci numbers which have a factor of 2.

Using other colours mark the numbers with factor 3, 4, 5, etc.

Fill in the following table:

2 is a factor of   3rd, 6th, 9th, ... Fibonacci numbers
3 is a factor of   — — — ...
4 is a factor of   — — — ...
5 is a factor of   — — — ...

What patterns do you notice?
Do numbers next to each other ever have the same factor?

4   Square and add two consecutive Fibonacci numbers. What do you notice about the result? Try it for several more pairs.

5   Which terms of the Fibonacci sequence do you get as a result of adding the squares of:
   (*a*) the 3rd and 4th terms;
   (*b*) the 5th and 6th terms;
   (*c*) the 100th and 101th terms?

Experiment 2

The Missing Area

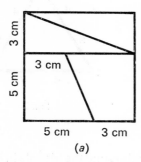
(*a*)

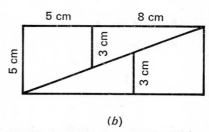
(*b*)

Fig. 10

Draw a square 8 cm by 8 cm and divide it up as shown in Figure 10 (*a*). Fit the pieces together to form the rectangle shown in Figure 10 (*b*).

What is the area of the square?
What is the area of the rectangle?
What happened to the missing square centimetre?

The square was 8 cm by 8 cm and the rectangle 5 cm by 13 cm; 5, 8 and 13 are consecutive Fibonacci numbers.

Choose any other 3 consecutive Fibonacci numbers, for example 13, 21 and 35. Draw a square 21 cm by 21 cm. Can you divide it up so that the pieces fit together to form a rectangle 13 cm by 35 cm?

157

Puzzle corner

1   Can you read this?

> 11 was 1 greyhound
>
> 22 was 12
>
> 1111 race
>
> 22112.

2   Copy Figure 1. Draw 4 straight line segments which pass through all 9 points without lifting your pencil from the paper and without tracing out any line twice.

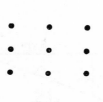

Fig. 1

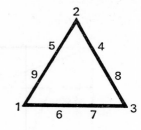

Fig. 2

3   The numbers 1 to 9 have been arranged around the triangle in Figure 2 so that the total of the numbers on each side comes to 17. See if you can rearrange them so that the total on each side is 20.

4   Work out the following:

$$9 \times 9 + 7 =$$

$$98 \times 9 + 6 =$$

$$987 \times 9 + 5 =$$

$$9876 \times 9 + 4 =$$

Can you extend the sequence?

5 Copy Figure 3 onto squared paper. Try to divide it into 3 pieces each of which is a net for an *open* cubical box.

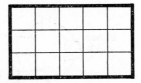

Fig. 3

6 Have you ever had trouble in folding a map? Then try this one. Fold up the map shown in Figure 4 so that the numbers are in order 1 to 8.

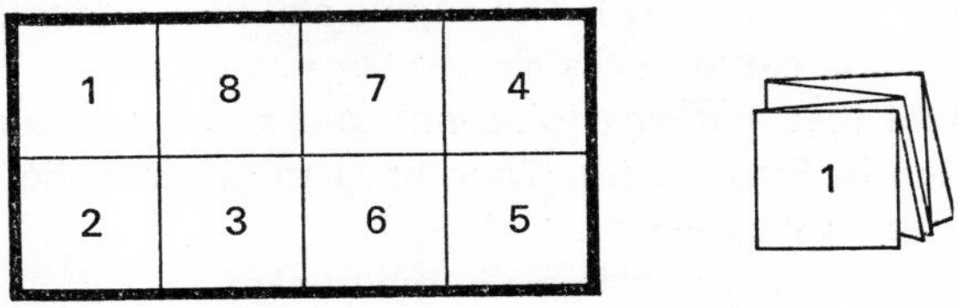

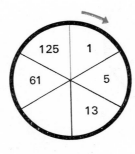

Fig. 4

7 Find the missing number in Figure 5.

Fig. 5

8 JAMES   Each letter stands for a number. If O represents 7 and
  −BOND   S represents 3, what do the other letters represent?
  ───────
   007

9   Figure 6 (*a*) shows a diagram of a shunting circuit at a railway station and the cattle truck and sheep truck are in the positions shown in this diagram.

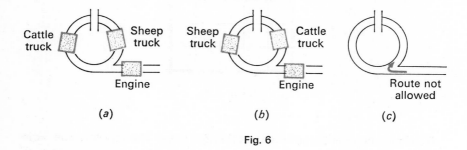

Fig. 6

The problem is to move the trucks so that they are in the positions shown in Figure 6 (*b*). The engine can pass under the bridge but the sheep and cattle trucks are too large to do so!

Note that neither engine nor trucks can go round the corner as shown in Figure 6 (*c*). They have to go past the corner and then reverse, or vice-versa.

Please keep the animals in the trucks!

10   Find the missing letter in Figure 7.

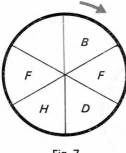

Fig. 7

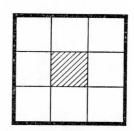

Fig. 8

11   Arrange the numbers 1, 2, 3, 4, 5, 7, 9, 10 in the empty squares in Figure 8 so that the sums of each row and column are always equal to 15.

Can you find another 8 numbers between 1 and 10 inclusive, so that when put in the box shape of Figure 8 the sums of each row and column are equal to 15?

12   Between two points, *A* and *B*, 99 km apart, there are 98 kilometre posts (see Figure 9). On how many of these posts are the two numbers made up of only two different digits? (e.g. 66 and 33, and 63 and 36.)

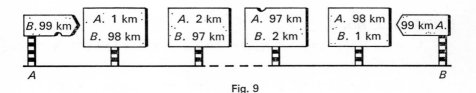

Fig. 9

13   It is required to arrange 4 objects in order of weight. A balance without any weights is available so that pairs of objects can be compared. How many weighings are required?

What is the maximum number of weighings that would be needed if you wanted to arrange 5 objects in order of weight?

14   Figure 10 shows 20 matches arranged in 2 groups so that the larger encloses three times the area inside the smaller. Can you now transfer 1 match from the larger group to the smaller and rearrange them both so that the 13 matches again enclose an area 3 times as large as that enclosed by the 7 matches?

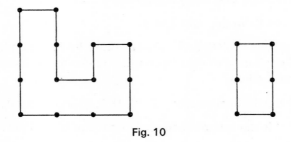

Fig. 10

If it is any help to you, 12 of the 20 matches are not touched at all and you are not allowed to bend or break the matches.

Revision exercises

Quick quiz, no. 3

1 What is the symmetry number for a rectangular box with a square base?

2 Does the point $(^-2, 3)$ lie on the line with equation $y = 2x + 7$?

3 Work out (a) $^-7 \times (3 + ^-8)$; (b) $(^-9 - ^-1) \div ^-4$.

4 What is 15% of £500?

5 What relation does the following set of points satisfy?
   $(^-3, 7)$, $(^-2, 5)$, $(^-1, 3)$, $(0, 1)$, $(1, ^-1)$, $(2, ^-3)$.

6 If the scale of a map is 1 to 50 000, state the distance in km represented by 10 cm on the map.

Quick quiz, no. 4

1 If $a = ^-1$, $b = 2$, $c = 1$, calculate $ab - c$.

2 How many axes of symmetry has a cube?

3 Divide £1 in the ratio 2 to 3.

4 Use Euler's relation, $F + V = E + 2$, to find the number of faces of a polyhedron with 4 vertices and 6 edges. What is the name of such a polyhedron?

5 What is the image set of $\{^-2, ^-1, 0, 1, 2\}$ under the mapping $x \rightarrow ^-2x$?

6 What is the size of each angle of a regular octagon?

Computation 2

1 $23 + 47 + 64 + 36 + 19 + 21$.

2 $(119 \times 57) - (117 \times 57)$.

3 $(41 \cdot 87 + 9 \cdot 84) \times 6 \cdot 3$.

4 $8284 \div 25$.

5 $0 \cdot 1 \times 0 \cdot 2 \times 0 \cdot 3 \times 0 \cdot 4 \times 0 \cdot 5$.

6 $(351 \cdot 86 \div 73) - 0 \cdot 83$.

Exercise D

1 The sizes of the two acute angles in a right-angled triangle are in the ratio 2 to 3. How big are they?

2 A transistor radio is priced for sale at £12·50. What would it cost if 10% discount were allowed off the marked price for paying cash?

3 Figure 1 represents the relation 'beat' for a set of 8 table tennis players in a knock-out tournament. The diagram is incomplete. Explain why, and complete it. Who won the tournament and who was the runner-up?

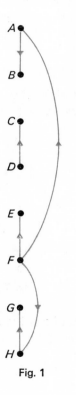

Fig. 1

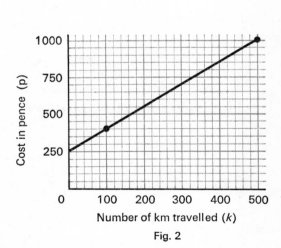

Fig. 2

4 A motorist calculated that the total weekly cost of running his car is given by $p = 1·5k + 250$ where k stands for the number of kilometres covered in the week and p the cost in pence.

(*a*) Use the graph of this relation (see Figure 2) to find the weekly cost if the motorist travels:

(i) 150 km;   (ii) 230 km;   (iii) 465 km.

163

(*b*) What is the weekly cost if the motorist does not use the car? Give possible reasons for this cost.

(*c*) What is the increase in cost for every 100 km travelled?

(*d*) What is the increase in cost for every 1 km travelled? Is there a connection between your answer and the relation between *p* and *k*?

5 Copy and complete this 'addition' table for odd and even numbers:

+	O	E
O		
E		

Write down the first 12 terms of the Fibonacci sequence and underneath each write O or E according to whether the terms of the sequence are odd or even. Comment on the pattern of O's and E's. Can you explain why it occurs?

Exercise E

1 A legacy of £6000 is to be divided between Bob and Carolyn in the ratio 1 to 2, but first death duties of 12% must be paid. How much do they each receive?

2 The rhombus, *ABCD*, is the cross-section of a prism.

(*a*) How many planes of symmetry has the prism?

(*b*) How many axes of symmetry and what is its order of rotational symmetry about each axis?

(*c*) What is its symmetry number?

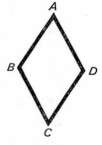

Fig. 3

3 The numbers in the fifth row of Pascal's triangle can be written

$$1, \quad \frac{4}{1}, \quad \frac{4 \times 3}{1 \times 2}, \quad \frac{4 \times 3 \times 2}{1 \times 2 \times 3}, \quad \frac{4 \times 3 \times 2 \times 1}{1 \times 2 \times 3 \times 4}.$$

Write in a similar manner the numbers in:

(*a*) the 6th row; (*b*) the 3rd row; (*c*) the 8th row.

4
$$(1+1)^2 = 1^2 + 1 + 1 + 1$$
$$(2+1)^2 = 2^2 + 2 + 2 + 1$$
$$(3+1)^2 = 3^2 + 3 + 3 + 1$$
$$(4+1)^2 = 4^2 + 4 + 4 + 1.$$

If $25^2 = 625$, use this pattern to find the value of 26^2.

5   If a car runs down a hill of slope 1 in 10, the distance *s* metres that it
    goes in *t* seconds is given roughly by the relation

$$s = \tfrac{1}{2}t^2.$$

Draw the graph of this relation by taking several values of *t* up to,
say, 24, and finding the corresponding distances. From your graph,
find how long it would be before the car crashed into a wall at the
bottom of the hill 200 m from where it was parked.

Exercise F

1   A triangle has vertices $A(1, 2)$, $B(1, 3)$ and $C(3, 3)$. Draw axes
    taking values of *x* and *y* from ⁻5 to 5 and plot the points *A*, *B*, *C*
    joining them up to make the triangle. Draw in the images of the
    triangle after it has been

    (*a*) reflected in $x = 0$;

    (*b*) reflected in $y = 0$;

    (*c*) rotated through 180° about (0, 0).

Indicate which image is which. If *ABC* is rotated into the position
with vertices at (2, 1), (4, 1) and (4, 2), draw this image and find
the centre of rotation. How can the pattern be completed?

2   I let a house through an estate agent whose fee is 7% of the rent.
    What do I receive in a year, if the rent is £12 a week?

3   Work out the following:
    (*a*) $9 - 8 - 6 - 3$;   (*b*) $(9 - 8) - (6 - 3)$;
    (*c*) $9 - (8 - 6) - 3$;   (*d*) $9 - 8 - (6 - 3)$.

4   *ABCDEF* is a regular hexagon, and
    ABXY is a square (see Figure 4).
    Find:

    (*a*) the size of angle *XBC*,
    (*b*) the size of angle *CXY*.

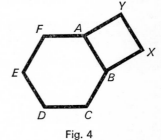

Fig. 4

If the length of *AB* is 2 cm, what is the ratio of the area of the square
to the area of the hexagon?

5 There are four factories situated in four towns A, B, C, D. The manager travels to inspect them from his home, O, by helicopter, and the journeys from O to A, B, C, D, respectively, can be described by the following vectors, the figures representing kilometres.

$$\mathbf{a} = \begin{pmatrix} 40 \\ 20 \end{pmatrix}, \quad \mathbf{b} = \begin{pmatrix} -50 \\ -20 \end{pmatrix}, \quad \mathbf{c} = \begin{pmatrix} 20 \\ -20 \end{pmatrix}, \quad \mathbf{d} = \begin{pmatrix} -40 \\ 30 \end{pmatrix}.$$

Draw a diagram to show the positions of all five places. If he sets out from home and visits A first, what vectors would represent his journeys from A to C then from C to B? Which is the shorter journey?

If he then sets out from B to go to D and by mistake travels on a course which could be described by the vector

$$\begin{pmatrix} 20 \\ 50 \end{pmatrix} \text{ instead of } \begin{pmatrix} 10 \\ 50 \end{pmatrix},$$

how could he get to D? Describe the journey which will take him home from D?

Exercise G

1 A quadrilateral $ABCD$ with vertices $A(1, 2)$, $B(\frac{1}{2}, 1)$, $C(3, 1)$ and $D(3, 2)$ is mapped by rotation onto quadrilateral $A'B'C'D'$ with vertices $A'(3\frac{1}{2}, 5\frac{1}{2})$, $B'(2\frac{1}{2}, 6)$, $C'(2\frac{1}{2}, 3\frac{1}{2})$, $D'(3\frac{1}{2}, 3\frac{1}{2})$. Find the centre of rotation using compasses and a ruler (no folding allowed).

2 If $E = \{$equilateral triangles$\}$,

   $I = \{$isosceles triangles$\}$,

   $O = \{$obtuse-angled triangles$\}$,

   $R = \{$right-angled triangles$\}$,

   draw, if possible, a triangle which belongs to each of the following sets.

   (a) $I \cap R$; (b) $O \cap R$; (c) $I \cap E$.

3 If $a = 5$ and $b = -2$, find the value of:

   (a) $3a + b$; (b) $3(a + b)$; (c) $a + 3b$;

   (d) $3a - b$; (e) $3(a - b)$; (f) $a - 3b$;

   (g) $\dfrac{a + b}{3}$; (h) $\frac{1}{3}(2a - b)$; (i) $\frac{1}{2}(3a + b)$.

4

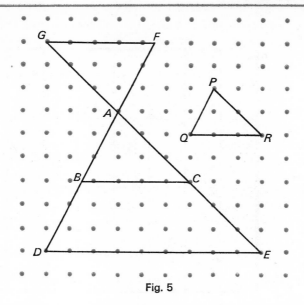

Fig. 5

Give the centre and scale factor of the enlargement which maps

(*a*) *ABC* onto *ADE*;   (*b*) *PQR* onto *ABC*;

(*c*) *AFG* onto *ABC*;   (*d*) *PQR* onto *AFG*;

(*e*) *PQR* onto *ADE*;   (*f*) *ADE* onto *PQR*;

(*g*) *ADE* onto *AFG*.

5   The table gives the number of absences in a Junior School for the winter term.

Number of Absences	Number of Children
0	22
1	14
2	69
3	3
4	50
5	3
6	87
7	0
8	52
9	0
10 and over	0
	Total 300

(*a*) Illustrate this information by means of a bar chart.

(*b*) What is the modal number of absences?

(*c*) What is the total number of absences?

(*d*) What is the mean number of absences?

(*e*) What percentage of children had three or more absences?

167

Exercise H

Across

2. $7.3 \div 0.01$.
5. The sum of the first seven prime numbers.
7. The sum of the prime factors of 572.
8. $(-4)^2 + {}^-5$.
10. The perimeter (in cm) of a regular hexagon of side 3 cm.
11. The number of planes of symmetry of a regular hexagonal prism.
12. $a(a+1)$ when $a = 12$.
13. $\dfrac{11}{12} \times \dfrac{12}{11}$.
14. 3^3.
15. The mean of 83, 87, 106, 91, 118, 110, 99, 98.
17. $24 \div \frac{3}{8}$.
19. The number of degrees in $\frac{1}{6}$ right-angle.
21. 150% of 150.

Down

1. How many 2 cm squares will fit into a 10 cm square?
3. The sum of the numbers in the sixth row of Pascal's triangle.
4. The first number which is a triangle and square number.
6. The ninth square number.
7. $2751 \div 100$ to 2 S.F.
9. 163_{ten} in base twelve.
10. $11_{\text{twelve}} \times 11_{\text{twelve}}$ in base ten.
14. The area (in cm²) of a right-angled triangle with sides 6 cm, 8 cm and 10 cm.
16. £100 less 9% of £100.
17. $a^2 + bc$ when $a = 5$, $b = 6$, $c = 7$.
18. 2.8×4.3 to 2 S.F.
20. 0.05 km in metres.